THE ROLE
OF THE
YANKEE
IN THE
OLD SOUTH

THE ROLE
OF THE
YANKEE
IN THE
OLD SOUTH

FLETCHER M. GREEN

MERCER UNIVERSITY LAMAR
MEMORIAL LECTURES, NO. 11

UNIVERSITY OF GEORGIA PRESS

ATHENS

©

1 9 7 2

UNIVERSITY OF GEORGIA PRESS

ISBN 0-8203-0233-3

LC 68-54086

Printed in the United States of America

Contents

Foreword

FLETCHER MELVIN GREEN IS ACCLAIMED BY HIS STUDENTS as the dean of Southern historians. Some of his students have contributed significant volumes to the Mercer University Lamar Memorial Lectures. It seemed fitting therefore in 1968 that Professor Green deliver the lectures for that year. He was at that time nearing retirement as Kenan Professor of History at the University of North Carolina. The following year as Harmsworth Professor of American History he lectured at Oxford and since that time has lived in Chapel Hill where as professor emeritus he continues active in writing and lecturing and inspiring students of Southern history.

Professor Green's lectures were on the general theme "The Role of the Yankee in the Old South," virtually an unexplored area in American history. The difficulty of the task he had set for himself did not discourage this meticulous scholar who has investigated every facet of Southern history. In addition to research previously done on his subject he spent several months as a Research Scholar at the Henry E. Huntington Library at San Marino, California, where he was able to gather much additional evidence to show that not only did Northerners come South before 1860—approximately 360,000—and contribute their proportionate share of influence in the region but also were, in turn, molded into the Southern pattern of thought, manners, and mores.

Professor Green would be the last to contend that the Yankee changed to any significant degree the Southern character; he, the Yankee, seems to have been more influenced by his environment than a molder of it. As Professor Green acknowledges, it would take much more research to prove to what degree the Yankee made the South what it was and is; but he organizes in a logical way an impressive list of names of Northerners who, individually, made worthy contributions to the economic, political, social, and cultural life of the South. And those Yankee leaders did, as Professor Green states, "exert an influence on Southern life far greater than is generally recognized." This study helps to weaken further an already weak theory that the Civil War resulted from a conflict between two distinctly different cultures.

Unfortunately, circumstances beyond his control caused a long delay in the publishing of Professor Green's lectures. On his return from Oxford the luggage containing his notes and manuscript was lost. That meant either giving up or attacking anew the task of gathering data and rewriting from the beginning. Professor Green is not one easily thwarted, and this finished product is proof of that. Now, with the eleventh volume, the Lamar lecture series has an unbroken line of annual publications dating back to 1957.

This volume gives Mercer University and the Lamar Memorial Lectures Committee another opportunity to pay tribute to Dorothy Eugenia Blount Lamar. It was her substantial legacy which makes possible these lectures and enables Mercer through the University of Georgia Press to publish them. It is the aim of the Lamar Lectures Committee to be faithful to the intent of the donor "to provide lectures of the very highest type of scholarship which will aid in the permanent preservation of the values of Southern culture, history and literature." Fletcher Green's lectures reach that goal.

Spencer B. King, Jr., Chairman
Lamar Memorial Lectures Committee

Preface

THE CONTROVERSY OVER SLAVERY WHICH DEVELOPED
between the North and South from 1830 to 1860 and cul-
minated in secession and Civil War left enmity between
Northerners and Southerners which lasted until late in the
twentieth century and, unfortunately, has not yet completely subsided. One feature of the controversy was the
charge that the word Yankee was applied to all Northerners by Southerners as a term of contempt and hatred.
Some Southerners still maintain that the Yankee was never
accepted socially in the Old South. Such a claim is not
true. In fact most Yankees who migrated to the South between the Union's gaining Independence from England
and the South's seceding from the Union made notable
contributions to every facet of Southern life and were generally accepted by Southerners. It was my intention in
these lectures to tell the story of the Yankees and to eval-
uate their role and contributions to Southern life.

I extend my appreciation to Mercer University and to the
Trustees of the Eugenia Dorothy Blount Lamar Memorial
Lectures for inviting me to deliver these lectures. I am deeply
indebted to Prof. Spencer B. King, Jr., and other members
of the Department of History who so graciously entertained
me and Mrs. Green while guests of Mercer University. My
thanks to Prof. James C. Bonner of Georgia State College at
Milledgeville and Dr. Judson C. Ward, Vice President of
Emory University, who so graciously took time from their

ix

important positions to attend and introduce me at the evening lectures. Finally I wish to thank the Huntington Library at San Marino, California, for appointing me a Research Scholar which enabled me to do research on Yankee activities in and contributions to the Old South.

INTRODUCTION

Who Were the Yankees?

THE LONG AND BITTER SECTIONAL CONTROVERSY OVER slavery in the United States, complicated by economic and political factors which brought on the Civil War, contributed to the myth that the people of the Northern and Southern states constituted two distinct and irreconcilable social and cultural groups, Yankees in the North and Cavaliers in the South. William Thompson of England, who toured the United States in the 1840s wrote: "The character of the Southern states for hospitality stands high, and it is not over rated. They are quite a distinct race from the 'Yankees.'" William R. Taylor has given us an excellent characterization of the two groups in his delightful book *Cavalier and Yankee: The Old South and American Character.* In it he pictures the Cavalier as gay, generous, indifferent to pecuniary matters, and familiar with polite culture and genteel ways, but weak, vacillating, self-indulgent, and vindictive. The Yankee, on the other hand, was thrifty, industrious, and ascetic, but hypocritical and mercenary. The Yankee, however, thought, of himself in terms of dignity, civic values, and idealism. John Neal, editor of the *Yankee,* wrote in 1828: "We Yankees value ourselves a good deal on our shrewdness; but . . . the word Yankee is no longer a term of reproach. It is getting to be a title of distinction, [and] our hope is to make it yet more respectable." A Yankee tutor in a South Carolina family took issue with Neal. He wrote in his autobiography that a Yankee peddler with "his Yankee honesty and Yankee tricks" was trying to sell "wooden nutmegs, horn flints, bass-

1

wood pumpkin seed, and sundry ingenious manufactures" of the North to the people in South Carolina.

Nathaniel Wright of Maine, urging New England young men to migrate to the South, told them in 1827 that they would easily find employment. The South, he said, "is a good field for enterprise. Yankees of talents and integrity generally succeed there." Seargent Smith Prentiss, one of those who followed Wright's advice and became eminently successful and highly popular with the people of Mississippi and the South generally, wrote in a memoir that "educated and trained in the habits of free Christian thought; deeply imbued with the spirit of virtuous intelligence and mental progress [New England Yankees] filled no small portion of the offices of trust and honor throughout the South."

In England the term *Yankee* was applied to all Americans, South as well as North, and "carried with it the implication of crass commercial dealings, shrewd bargaining, and even sharp practices." By 1815 the word *Yankee* in England evoked a general image of uncouth and curious rustics whose energies were almost exclusively given over to pursuit of economic gain. Southerners attempted to free themselves from this stigma. For instance, William C. Preston, while traveling in England, insisted in a conversation with an English lady that he was a "Virginian, not a Yankee." But she replied: "Aye, a proud Virginian. But to us you are all Yankees, rascals who cheat the whole world." Northerners also resented the charge that they were greedy, selfish, grasping, and lacking in genteel taste, intellectual distinction, and private as well as public decorum. Henry David Thoreau wrote that "the Yankee, though undisciplined, had this advantage at least, that he is especially a man who, everywhere and under all circumstances, is fully resolved to better his condition."

The origin of the term Yankee is uncertain. Charles O. F. Thompson in *A History of the Declaration of Independence* says that "Yankee Doodle a famous song of the American Revolution" was an adaptation from "Nankee Doodle" sung by

Oliver Cromwell's troops in the English civil wars of the 1660s. In 1775, when poorly trained and poorly equipped troops from New England joined British forces at Albany, New York, an English surgeon wrote an American version of the earlier song which he called "Yankee Doodle" in derision of the Albany townspeople. Later, during the American Revolution, "the American Army adapted the song as their own and played it incessantly." Yankee Doodle, described as "a simple young yokel from the country visited the Army" and sang:

> Father and I went down to camp
> Along with Captain Good'ng
> And there we saw the men and boys
> As thick as hasty Puddin.

The verse is followed by the chorus:

> Yankee Doodle, keep it up,
> Yankee Doodle Dandy,
> Mind the music and the step,
> And with the girls be handy.

The British troops applied the term *Yankee* to the New Englanders first as a contemptuous nickname, second as a simple descriptive word, and finally in the twentieth century as a respectable designation of all Americans, especially the American troops during World War I, whom they welcomed with the song "The Yanks Are Coming." Southerners never willingly accepted the term *Yankee* when applied to themselves and, during the bitter controversy over slavery and abolition, began to speak contemptuously of the New England Yankees. When the Civil War came, Southerners generally applied the term *Yankee* to all resident Northerners. However, Southerners welcomed Yankees who had settled in the South. Scores of planters hired Northern tutors and governesses to teach their sons and daughters. In 1752 some 350 New England Puritans moved to South Carolina where a goodly number of them became planters and slaveholders. Another group moved to Midway, Georgia, where they became rice and indigo planters. Incidentally, most of these groups became ardent champions of slavery.

A colony of New Englanders settled in Fairfax County, Virginia, in the early 1840s, where they were welcomed by the Virginians. The Petersburg Agricultural Society urged Yankees to settle in that area, and John Hamden Pleasants, editor of the Richmond *Whig*, declared: "An infusion of a little Yankee industry and capital into the arteries of Virginia will produce a beneficial effect. We have seen it done recently in Fairfax." Eli J. Capell, a wealthy planter and noted agricultural reformer of Mississippi, wrote in 1852: "I wish that more of our Northern farmers and mechanics could be induced to settle among us. They would add sobriety, thrift, and better methods of agriculture to the community." There is little evidence to support the view that Southerners were hostile to Northern settlers. Yankees were quickly assimilated and almost lost their identity. They entered into the varied careers open to Southerners, and a large percentage of them rose to prominence in agriculture, business, industry, education, ministry, law, and politics. And many of them became slaveholders.

The rise of the radical abolition crusade in the 1830s, however, caused Southerners to develop a critical attitude toward Northerners who were outspoken in opposition to slavery, and they began to question resident Yankees in regard to their views, especially those who were thought to be soft on the slavery issue. For example, Enos W. Newton, a native of Vermont who had settled in Virginia, became widely known for his liberal views which he expressed in the *Kanawha Republican* of which he was the editor. He championed temperance reform, internal improvements at public expense, and free public schools. He also advocated a protective tariff which was unpopular in Virginia, but he dodged any discussion of slavery. A rival Virginia editor charged Newton with backing free soil doctrines and with circulating incendiary antislavery publications. Whereupon Newton replied that he had resided in Virginia since 1817, had married a Southern girl, and that his children had been born in Virginia. "Upon the subject of slavery [he said] we never entertain any opinion not in accordance with those entertained by the intelligent slaveholders themselves." Newton weathered the storm and was generally accepted in his community. Slavery was the key issue in the acceptance of the Yankee after the rise of the abolition crusade, and Northerners who resided in the South and opposed the institution were socially ostracized, persecuted, and driven from the South, while those who conformed to the Southern view of slavery were warmly welcomed and socially accepted.

The United States census of 1860 shows that there were upwards of 360,000 Yankees living in the Old South. How many Yankees had come to the South since the American colonists had won their independence from England, lived out their allotted span of years, made their contributions to their day and generation, and had passed on to their reward there is no way of knowing, for the census figures prior to 1850 are not only inadequate, but also incorrect. Because of the short life expectancy during that period one might hazard a guess that the total number of Yankees who moved to the South between 1776 and 1860 would have been above half a million. Some of them had moved to the South in the maturity of years with established reputations in their chosen fields of endeavor; some were children; and others, probably a large majority, were young men and women who sought opportunity in a new land. Some became dissatisfied and returned to the North, and some few had been driven out because of their outspoken opposition to slavery. Those who remained made a place for themselves in various walks of life as farmers, overseers, and planters; common laborers, skilled artisans, inventors, and contractors; merchants, shippers, bankers, industrialists, and railroad magnates; professionals, such as tutors, college professors and presidents, lawyers, doctors, ministers, and scientists; journalists and men of letters; and politicians, governmental officials, and diplomats. Many of them made significant contributions to their adopted state and region; others made national and international reputations. A goodly number of the young men made significant contributions to the Confederacy. For example some fifty Northern-born Yankees attained the rank of general in the Confederate Army and a large number attained lesser rank. Overall the Yankees exerted an influence on Southern life far greater than is generally recognized and out of proportion to their numbers.

ONE

Government and Politics

1. The Federal Period

FROM THE DECLARATION OF INDEPENDENCE, JULY 4, 1776, to the secession of the eleven Southern states from the Union in 1860–1861, Yankees who migrated to the South played significant roles in government and politics, in Congress, and in the state legislatures. Among them were fourteen signers of the Declaration of Independence, one signer of the Articles of Confederation, and four signers of the Constitution of the United States. Virginia had no Yankee representative in any of these important bodies, and South Carolina sent only one Yankee to the Continental Congress and none to the other bodies. The probable explanation can be found in the fact that the inhabitants of these two colonies with their greater wealth had been able to send their sons to the English Inns of Court for education and training in politics. Hence they were well supplied with local leaders. Some two hundred transplanted Yankees were elected to the Congress of the United States by the Southern states before 1860, many of whom were highly influential in the passage of important legislation. Southern Yankees sat on the benches of both the Supreme and inferior courts, some served in the president's cabinet, and others as ministers to foreign countries where they negotiated important treaties. Southern Yankee officers served in the United States Army and Navy and helped Federal troops to victory in the War of 1812, the war with Mexico, and numerous Indian conflicts. In addition more than fifty Yankees were generals in the Confederate States

7

Army during the Civil War. Yankees were equally important in state government and politics. They served as legislators, governors, and judges in the courts of all the Southern
states. They were leaders in the fight for democratic reform,
the development of internal improvements, and the establishment of state universities, public schools, private academies, and church-related colleges throughout the South. As
a group the Southern Yankees were generally educated, well
trained, and able to influence thought and action. They
made significant contributions to almost every facet of
Southern life. Brief sketches of the Yankee leaders in the
federal period will indicate the interests, activities, and accomplishments of selected leaders in the organization and
development of that period.

Several Yankees were prominent in North Carolina's history. Joseph Hewes was born in New Jersey in 1730, moved
to Pennsylvania where he became a prosperous merchant
and shipper, and then moved to Edenton, North Carolina,
in 1763. There he became a member of the Committee of
Correspondence, a delegate to all five of North Carolina's
provincial congresses where he served on the Committee of
Claims, the committee to prepare a plan of confederation
and chairman of the Committee on Marine. As director of
naval affairs he appointed John Paul Jones a naval officer
and supplied him with his first fighting ship. Hewes was a
signer of the Declaration of Independence and, according to
John Adams, was the deciding influence in the adoption of
that document. Adams wrote Thomas Jefferson as follows:
"You know that the Unanimity of the States on independence depended on Joseph Hewes, and was determined by
him."

William Hooper was born in Boston in 1742 and was
graduated from Harvard College in 1760. He moved to
North Carolina in 1764 and was appointed attorney general
and elected to the General Assembly in 1773. He was a
member of the first North Carolina Provincial Congress

which in turn elected him to the Continental Congress where he served from 1774 to 1777. Hooper was an ardent advocate of independence but was absent when the vote to adopt the Declaration of Independence was taken; he returned to sign the Declaration of Independence on August 2, 1776. Hooper was a member of the North Carolina House of Commons from 1777 to 1782 and in 1784. Hooper was appointed a member of the United States commission in 1786 which was formed to decide on the territorial rights between New York and New Jersey.

Hugh Williamson was born in Pennsylvania in 1735, and was graduated from the University of Pennsylvania in 1757. He studied medicine at Edinburgh, Scotland, and at the University of Utrecht, where he received the doctor of medicine degree. Returning to Pennsylvania, Williamson served as professor of mathematics at the university from 1760 to 1763. He removed to North Carolina in 1776 and was appointed surgeon general of North Carolina troops during the Revolution and supervised the inoculation of the state troops against smallpox. Williamson represented North Carolina in the Continental Congress in the Annapolis convention of 1786 where the first steps toward the adoption of a constitutional union were taken and in the Constitutional Convention of 1787 where he played an important role in the framing of the United States Constitution. He was also a member of the North Carolina convention called to ratify the Constitution of the United States. The first assembly of the convention failed to act and Williamson, a zealous advocate of the Constitution, wrote and published an essay, "Remarks on the New Plan of Government," which had considerable influence on ratification of the Constitution in the second convention. Williamson also published numerous scientific papers, including one "Observations on Navigable Canals" in which he advocated the building of canals for transportation purposes. This paper had considerable influence on the construction of internal improvements in the state. Williamson also published two important books of the period: *Observations on the Climate of Different Parts of America* and a *History of North Carolina* in two volumes.

Alexander Martin was born in New Jersey in 1740 and was educated at Princeton University. He moved to North Carolina in 1760 and later served in the house of commons and two provincial congresses. Martin was a colonel in the Revolutionary Army under General Washington at the battle of Germantown, where he was charged with cowardly conduct, arrested and court-martialed, but he was acquitted. Martin resigned from the army in 1777 and returned to North Carolina, where he served in the state senate for seven years and as speaker for four years. He was acting governor of the state for two years and governor for seven years. He urged the state to engage in manufacturing and to use convict labor for developing internal improvements. Martin served as a member of the United States House of Representatives for six years and of the Senate from 1793 to 1799. His support of and vote for the alien and sedition acts was very unpopular with North Carolinians and he was defeated in the next election.

The North Carolina delegation in the Constitutional Convention of 1787 and the United States Congress in the decade of the 1790s has been characterized as made up of "respectable characters rather than brilliant men." They did, however, serve their day and generation well.

Georgia's chief Yankee leaders during the early years of the new nation were Lyman Hall, Abraham Baldwin, and Nathan Brownson. Hall was born in Connecticut in 1724, was graduated from Yale College, entered the ministry, and later studied medicine. He moved to Georgia in 1756 and became a wealthy rice planter, but he continued in the ministry. Hall was elected to the second Provincial Council of Georgia in 1775, where he was characterized "as the hottest advocate of independence in Georgia." The Georgia delegates who had been elected by the first provincial coun-

cil to the Continential Congress refused to attend; whereupon Hall, with other ardent advocates of independence,
requested South Carolina to accept a delegate from the
Georgia parish to accompany her delegation to the congress.
That the South Carolinians refused to do, but they did re-
commend the parish delegate, Lyman Hall, to the second
Continental Congress. He attended the congress and participated in its discussion but did not vote. When Georgia's
second provincial council sent a delegation of three to the
congress it added Hall's name to the group because of his
enthusiasm for and leadership in the fight for independence.
In fact so vigorous had been his campaign against British
rule that her troops burned his home and ravaged his plantation. Hall had the honor and satisfaction to be one of the
three signers from Georgia. Hall was elected governor of
Georgia in 1783, and he recommended that the legislature
set aside forty thousand acres of land for an institution of
higher learning. This recommendation resulted later in the
chartering of the University of Georgia.

Abraham Baldwin was born in Connecticut in 1754, was
graduated from Yale in 1772, and was a tutor in that institution for three years. He served as a chaplain in the Revolutionary Army from 1779 to 1783. He removed to Georgia in
1784 and was elected to the state legislature. He served in the
Continental Congress from 1785 to 1788, the Constitutional
Convention in 1787, the United States House of Representatives from 1789 to 1799, and the Senate from 1799 to 1807.
Baldwin was a member of the commission which made a
final settlement in 1802 of Georgia's western lands. Georgia
agreed to give up all her territory west of the Chattahoocheee
River and in return the United States agreed "to secure for
Georgia all Indian lands within the state at the United
State's expense . . . as early as the same can be peaceably
obtained at reasonable terms." This treaty has been characterized as a "happy settlement, equitable alike to the United
States and Georgia, largely accomplished through the con-

ciliatory and persuasive counsels of Baldwin." As a member
of the Constitutional Convention, Baldwin opposed equal
representation of the states in the Senate, but convinced that
the small states would withdraw from the convention if this
was not granted, he brought about a tie vote on this provision
by changing his vote and was largely responsible for the
compromise that "Representation and direct Taxes shall be
apportioned among the several States . . . according to
their respective numbers . . . including . . . free Persons . . .
and three fifths of all other Persons," and that "each State
shall have two Senators." He strenuously opposed any grant
of power to the federal government to abolish slavery, saying:
"Georgia is decided on this point." He also opposed the
assumption of state debts by the United States. Later in
Congress he was to oppose the alien and sedition acts and to
support James Madison's views on tariff and custom duties.
Baldwin was unquestionably the ablest and most influential
member of the Georgia delegation, but he was not, as Joel
Barlow of Massachusetts described him, "the Father of the
Constitution."

Nathan Brownson, the third member of the Georgia delegation in the Continental Congress, was born in Connecticut in 1742, was graduated from Yale College in 1761,
studied medicine and then moved to Georgia in 1764 where
he began to practice his profession. He soon took a deep
interest in the quarrel with England and was elected to the
provincial council in 1775 and the Continental Congress in
1776. He served as a surgeon in the Revolutionary Army.
After the war Brownson was a delegate to the Georgia convention which ratified the United States Constituion and to
the Georgia convention which framed the state constituion.
He closed his political career as speaker of the Georgia senate
in 1791.

Four Maryland Yankees were active and influential in the
establishment and development of the state and national
governments from the beginning of the Revolution until well

into the nineteenth century. Two of them, James McHenry of Pennsylvania and Luther Martin of New Jersey, were of great importance. McHenry studied medicine with the distinguished Dr. Benjamin Rush of Philadelphia and served as a surgeon in the Revolutionary Army. He was a member of General Lafayette's staff and secretary to General Washington. After the war McHenry was a member of the Continental Congress from 1783 to 1786, and the Constitutional Convention of 1787, and he was a signer of the Articles of Confederation and of the United States Constitution. McHenry was secretary of war in the cabinet of Presidents George Washington and John Adams. He served in the Maryland state legislature from 1781 to 1786 and again from 1791 to 1796. Despite his almost continuous service to state and nation he found time to help organize and to serve as the first president of the Bible Society of Maryland.

Luther Martin, a native of New Jersey and a graduate of Princeton University, moved to Maryland in 1766, studied law under George Wythe of Virginia, was the first attorney general of his adopted state, and one of the most influential lawyers in the United States. He was elected to the Continental Congress of 1785 and the Constitutional Convention of 1787. In these bodies he distinguished himself as a representative of the interests of the small states and a champion of the debtors, small farmers, and working men. He also supported the claims of the small states in regard to western lands. However, he favored a strong court and held that the question of determining the "constitutionality of the laws of Congress will come before the Judges in the proper official capacity. In this capacity they have a negative on the laws [of Congress]." Oddly enough, in view of his states' rights philosophy, Martin drafted the provision of the Constitution which was modified to read that "this Constitution and the Laws of the United States . . . and all Treaties . . . shall be the Supreme Law of the Land; and the Judges in every State shall be bound thereby; any Thing in the Constitution or laws of any State to the Contrary notwithstanding." Believing that the Constitution would restrict the state governments and limit the rights of the people, Martin refused to sign the document and went back to Maryland to urge the people to reject it. On leaving the convention he told a colleague from Maryland, "I'll be hanged if ever the people of Maryland agree to it." To which his friend replied, "I advise you to stay in Philadelphia lest you should be hanged." Martin misjudged the people of his adopted state; they did ratify the Constitution. The law was Martin's chief love. He was counsel for Judge Samuel Chase in his impeachment trial, and he argued the case of *McCulloch* v. *Maryland* before the United States Supreme Court in 1819. In the latter case his argument centered chiefly around the question of states rights. He was attorney general of Maryland for thirty-one years and the recognized leader of the American Bar Association.

Little Delaware was represented by four Yankees, all born in Pennsylvania, and each of whom served in one or more of the key bodies which called into being and helped to establish the United States and to organize its government. Each of these men played an important role in the political life of the American nation in its early years. They were Thomas McKean, the Gunning Bedfords, Jr. and Sr., and Samuel Wharton.

McKean, born in 1734 and educated at the Middle Temple in London, moved to Delaware in 1755, where he held numerous posts of honor and trust. He was a delegate to the Stamp Act Congress, a member of the state house of delegates from 1762 to 1775, speaker of that body and of the Continental Congress from 1774 to 1783, and president of the congress in 1781. He was a signer of the Declaration of Independence in 1777 and was the first to correct the popular impression that the declaration had been signed on July 4, 1776. Later, McKean was to prove that no one signed on that day. He helped to draft the constitution of Delaware in

1776 and was a member and speaker of the state house in 1776–1777. He was a member of the United States Constitutional Convention of 1787, and later served as chief justice of the Delaware Supreme Court.

Gunning Bedford, Sr., was born in Philadelphia in 1742 and moved to Delaware as a young man. He saw service as a colonel in the Revolutionary Army, was wounded at the battle of White Plains, and was appointed muster-master general in 1776. He was a member of the state legislature, serving in the house from 1784 to 1786, in the senate in 1788, and as a member of the Privy Council from 1783 to 1790. Bedford was elected to the Continental Congress in 1786 and of the state ratification convention of 1787 in which he was an ardent supporter of ratifying the Constitution of the United States. He was a longtime champion of public education and was influential in the establishment of the Delaware Public School System. Bedford was elected governor of Delaware in 1796 and died in office in 1797.

Bedford, Junior (cousin of Bedford, Senior), was born in Philadelphia in 1747, was graduated from Princeton University and moved to Delaware in 1771, where he began the practice of law in 1772. Bedford served as a member of both houses of the Delaware legislature and was a delegate to the Continental Congress, the Annapolis convention, the Delaware Constitutional Convention, and the Philadelphia convention of 1787 which framed the Constitution of the United States. In the latter body he proposed equal representation of the states in the Senate, short presidential terms of office, and a strong legislative body. He was appointed the first judge of the United States District Court of Delaware in 1798. He died in 1812. Strange as it may seem, none of these three Delaware statesmen is mentioned in the major work on the fathers of the Constitution or in one of the most widely used college textbooks on the history of the United States to 1865.

If Virginia and South Carolina had no Yankees who

played prominent roles in the winning of independence and the establishment of the United States government, they did have Yankees who supplemented their native leaders. John Peter Gabriel Muhlenberg of Virginia and David Ramsey of South Carolina are excellent examples of this group. Muhlenberg, son of Henry M. Muhlenberg, a doctor of divinity who was the patriarch of the Lutheran church in the United States, was born in Pennsylvania in 1750 and educated for the ministry in Germany. On his return he established himself at Woodstock, Virginia, and later went to London, where he was ordained as an Episcopal minister. He became an intimate friend of George Washington and served on the Virginia Committee of Correspondence in 1775. At the outbreak of the Revolution he offered his services to the state and was commissioned a colonel in the Eighth Virginia Regiment. He preached his last sermon at Woodstock with his clerical robe covering his military uniform. He closed his sermon as follows: "There is a time for all things—a time to preach, and a time to pray, but there is also a time to fight, and that time has now come." After pronouncing the benediction, he pulled off his clerical robe disclosing his military uniform. Theatrical and sensational his action was, but it also had magical results. His parishioners rallied in numbers to the standard of their minister-colonel. He fought in the battles at Brandywine, Germantown, Monmouth, and Yorktown and was mustered out of service as a major general. After the close of the war he returned to Pennsylvania, was elected to Congress, and ended his career as collector of the port of Philadelphia.

David Ramsey was born in Pennsylvania in 1749, was graduated from Princeton University, and received a doctor of medicine degree from the University of Pennsylvania. He moved to South Carolina in 1774. He was one of the most versatile men of his day and made significant contributions to his adopted state and the nation in many fields. Ramsey served in both houses of the South Carolina legislature and was president of the senate. He was a delegate to the Continental Congress and a member of the South Carolina convention which ratified the United States Constitution. He was a surgeon in the Charleston battalion during the Revolution, introduced vaccination in South Carolina, and supervised the nitre works for the state. He saw and condemned the evils of slavery, declaring that the Negro was degraded not by nature but by slavery. Ramsey introduced a bill in the state legislature in 1785 to end the importation of slaves, and he published an article on the evils of importation in 1791. It should be noted, however, that he modified his attack on slavery after his marriage to an heiress possessed of a plantation and a large slave-labor force. Ramsey advocated state support of education at both the public school and college level. He helped to organize the Medical Society of South Carolina in 1789 and advocated the drainage of the South Carolina lowland swamps as a sanitary measure. As a historian he advocated the collection and preservation of source materials. In his own writing Ramsey attempted to be fair and impartial, but he was not averse to giving his own views and interpretation of his finding. His outlook and point of view as a historian was nationalistic, not state or regional. Ramsey's published works include *Review of . . . Medicine in the Eighteenth Century, Life of George Washington, History of South Carolina* in two volumes, *History of the American Revolution, History of the United States* in three volumes, and numerous articles and orations.

Three Yankees played significant roles in organizing the first new territories of the Old Southwest. John Todd settled in Virginia in 1775 but soon moved beyond the Appalachian Mountains and helped to organize the Transylvania colonial legislature. He was one of the first two representatives sent to the Virginia legislature from Kentucky County. As a member of the legislature he secured a grant of land for schools in the western district and also introduced a bill, which failed to pass, providing for the emancipation of slaves. Todd marched with George Rogers Clark to Vincennes and Kaskaskia and was commissioned by Gov. Patrick Henry to organize the Illinois County. He was killed at the battle of Blue Licks in 1782. Joseph Anderson, a native of Pennsylvania, served as a major and paymaster in the Revolutionary Army, and moved to Delaware where he began the practice of law. President George Washington appointed Anderson judge of the territory south of the Ohio River, which post he held from 1791 to 1796. Anderson was elected to the United States Senate from the new state of Tennessee in 1797 and served until 1815. He was appointed the first comptroller of the United States Treasury and served in that post from 1815 to 1836. David Holmes, born in Pennsylvania in 1770, moved to Virginia, where he studied law at the College of William and Mary. He served as attorney of Rockingham County and was a member of Congress from Virginia from 1797 to 1809. President James Madison appointed Anderson governor of the territory of Mississippi, a post he held from 1809 to 1817. Anderson presided over the Mississippi Constitutional Convention of 1817 which, under his leadership, drafted a liberal and democratic constitution for the new state. Anderson served as governor of Mississippi from 1817 to 1820 and as United States senator from Mississippi from 1820 to 1825. Anderson and Holmes, in addition to guiding Tennessee and Mississippi to statehood and the adoption of state constitutions that were, for that period, very democratic, also made important contributions to educational advancement in their respective states, and each served as trustee of the first college established in his state.

2. The Middle Period

Yankee leaders in the South from 1815 to 1860, a time generally called the middle period of American history, increased in number far above that of the days of the founding fathers. Furthermore, as the fields of their service became more widespread, their contributions to Southern life became more conspicuous. At the same time the bitter sectional controversy over slavery and state rights caused Yankee leaders to stand out more clearly than they had during the early years of the republic. One should bear in mind, however, that there was no organized block of Yankee leaders. In politics Yankees were divided between Whigs and Democrats just as were the native Southerners; hence it is impossible to deal with the Yankees as a group. Also their contributions to the Old South must be assessed and evaluated on an individual basis. The discussion will, however, generally be a chronological one. Representatives of the many Yankees in the South have been chosen so as to give a balanced view of Whig and Democratic leaders from the various Southern states.

Samuel Smith was born in Pennsylvania in 1752 and moved to Maryland in 1760. His career bridges the gap of Yankee leadership from the days of the founding fathers to that of the middle period. Smith served in the Revolutionary Army, helped suppress the Pennsylvania Whiskey Rebellion of 1793 to 1803, and was a member of the United States Senate from 1803 to 1815 and from 1822 to 1833. Somewhere along the road he shifted from Federalist to Republican in his party affiliation, but he opposed the nomination of James Madison for president by the Republicans in 1808. He was the author of the nonimportation legislation of 1806, but he opposed the Macon Bill Number Two which restored commercial intercourse with both England and France.

Henry Adams Bullard was born in Massachusetts and educated at Harvard College. He practiced law in Boston, moved to Philadelphia, and in 1812 joined a group of Americans who went to Mexico with the intent of joining the revolutionaries in their effort to gain Mexican independence. Bullard settled in New Orleans and began the practice of law in 1813. With a command of the French language he worked to familiarize himself with the basic principles of the Napoleonic Code. He was successful and rose rapidly in the legal profession. He served as district judge from 1822 to 1830 and judge of the state supreme court from 1834 to 1842. Bullard's service on the bench was of great importance in the reconciliation of French and English law. He was a Whig in politics and served in the United States Congress from 1830 to 1834 and again from 1850 to 1851. After his retirement from the supreme court in 1842 Bullard became professor of law at the University of Louisiana, now Tulane University. He was instrumental in the establishment of the Louisiana Historical Society and served as its first president in 1846.

Amos Kendall was born in Massachusetts in 1789. He was graduated from Dartmouth College and moved to Kentucky in 1814 where he became a tutor in the home of Henry Clay. He found young Tom Clay, whom he was tutoring, a very obstreperous youth, who, wrote Kendall, "fought me like a tiger and cursed me with all his might. You damned Yankee rascal, you have been trying to make yourself of great importance among the ladies this evening." Unwilling to bear such treatment, Kendall turned to journalism and established the *Argus of Western America* in Frankfort. In this paper he published "Sketches of Education for the Consideration of the People of Kentucky Particularly the Members of the Next Legislature." In these essays Kendall took the position that there could be no sound republican government unless a majority of the people could read and that natural ability without learning was not sufficient for leadership—the people must also be enlightened. Kendall noted that the state legislators were almost exclusively lawyers and asked why this was so. He gave his own answer: "Because farmers, laborers, and mechanics do not read." Kendall praised the state legislators for having made appropriations for Transylvania University but regretted that *"they had left undone that which they ought to have done,* [namely] *the establishment of free public Schools."* Kendall urged the legislature to take measures to raise the great mass of the people as nearly as possible to the favored sons of the rich. "In short we would establish a system of public schools, co-existent with the State which should be open to the poor as well as the rich, and disburse the blessings of . . . a common education to every citizen." Kendall was one of the first advocates of public education in Kentucky and was influential in securing an act to set apart one-half of the profits of the state-owned Bank of the Commonwealth as a public school fund.

Kendall supported Andrew Jackson for president in the election of 1828 and was rewarded by an appointment as an auditor in the Treasury Department. He became a member of Jackson's Kitchen Cabinet and an adviser and speech writer for the president. In his newspapers, the *Expositor* and the *Union Democrat,* he vigorously opposed the protective tariff and supported Jackson's war on the the United States bank. Kendall was vitally interested in the care and education of the deaf and dumb and was active in the establishment of the Columbian Institution for the Deaf and Dumb in Washington, D.C. He gave the ground on which the school was established and was instrumental in getting the United States government to give financial support to indigent students. Disturbed by the growing dissension over the question of slavery in the territories and the threat of secession by the Southern states, Kendall proposed a plan to President James Buchanan which he hoped would calm the passions of the people and bring peace to the nation. Pointing out that there had been disunionists in the South since the nullification crisis and that there were now disunionists among the abolitionists in the North, he suggested that the president "assume and inflexibly maintain two positions: First. The Federal Union shall be preserved, as organized by the Constitution, in its letter and spirit. Second. Inflexible opposition to any further agitation of the subject of slavery in the Territories." But he gave no method of enforcing the plan. He wrote a series of twelve articles against secession in 1860 with the Jackson slogan on nullification, "The Federal Union Must Be Preserved." When the Civil War came, he gave his property in Washington to the federal government.

Edward Livingston, born in New York in 1764 and a graduate of Princeton University, had been a representative in Congress and a bitter opponent of the alien and sedition acts before he removed to Louisiana in 1803. During the War of 1812 he had been successful in getting the non-English inhabitants of New Orleans to join forces with the native Americans in resisting the English, and he was a trusted adviser and aide-de-camp to General Jackson. As a citizen of Louisiana he served in the state legislature, as a representative in the United States Congress, as secretary of state in President Andrew Jackson's cabinet, and as minister plenipotentiary to France. As secretary of state he was one of President Jackson's confidential advisers and prepared for him several able state papers, including the Nullification Proclamation of 1832. As minister to France, Livingston was influential in bringing about peaceful settlement of the thorny problem of the spoliation claims which had been a bone of contention between the two countries since the close of the War of 1812. But his more enduring fame rests on his work in legal reform in Louisiana. The four codes of crime and punishment, procedure, evidence, and prison discipline, known in Europe as Livingston's Code, were never fully adopted in Louisiana, but they were reprinted in England, France, and Germany and have been studied throughout the world. Sir Henry Maine, England's great legal reformer, described Livingston as "the first legal genius of modern times." Livingston was elected to membership in the French Academy and lectured before that body. François Mignet, noted French historian, wrote after Livingston's death in 1836: "By the death of Mr. Livingston America has lost her most powerful intellect, the [French] Academy one of its most illustrious members, and humanity one of her most zealous benefactors." Roscoe Pound, longtime professor of law at Harvard University and a great legal philosopher in his own right, said that Livingston should rank with Cesare Beccaria, Italy's great criminologist, and Alexis de Tocqueville, France's great philosopher in jurisprudence, as one of the three greatest legal reformers of modern times.

John Slidell, born in New York in 1793, was a graduate of Columbia University. He failed as a merchant in New York City and removed to New Orleans in 1819 where he made a fortune in business. He then entered politics as a Democrat and served in the Louisiana state senate and in the United States House of Representatives. In the latter body he was an ardent champion of tariff reduction, except in the case of sugar, since the Louisiana sugar growers opposed a tariff reduction on that product. By shrewd political management, "wire pulling," and the control of "floaters," Slidell assured James K. Polk's victory in Louisiana, and as a reward President Polk appointed Slidell United States commissioner to Mexico. He failed in his mission to adjust the Texas boundary dispute, the United States claims against Mexico, and the purchase of New Mexico and California. The United States military victory and the acquisition of the territory by treaty prevented Slidell's loss of face, and he turned his efforts to the construction of a New Orleans–Nashville railroad which he financed through the sale of bonds in Europe. He was elected to the United States Senate in 1852 where he championed the Southern position on slavery in Kansas and the effort to acquire Cuba from Spain. Slidell cast his lot with the Confederate States of America in 1860. He wrote S. L. M. Barlow, a business partner, on November 20, 1860, explaining his attitude: "I think it best that Lincoln has succeeded. It brings the matter to an issue at the best time and the best circumstances. The most skeptical will now be convinced that the South is in earnest and you may consider the Union as already dissolved for I have no hope of the North retracing its steps. We have many true friends there from whom it will be painful to separate but self preservation is the supreme law" of the land. He was appointed one of the Confederate commissioners to France in

1861, but his success was limited. After the defeat of the Confederacy in 1865, Slidell chose to remain in France.

Three of the many Yankees who played significant roles in Mississippi politics have been singled out for consideration. They are John A. Quitman, an extremist; Robert J. Walker, a statesman who refused to go with the South in secession; and Seargent S. Prentiss, one of the noted orators of his day.

Quitman was a native of New York, where he was born in 1798. He was graduated from Hartwick Seminary and moved to Mississippi in 1824. He entered politics and quickly won general favor with the people. He was elected to the state legislature and was a member of the state constitutional convention of 1832 where he participated in drafting a very democratic constitution. Quitman served as a judge of the state superior court, of the high court of appeals, and as chancellor of state from 1825 to 1835. He was an ardent supporter of John C. Calhoun's theory of the right of a state to nullify acts of Congress which it considered unconstitutional, and after the Panic of 1837 he favored the repudiation of Mississippi's state bonds. As governor of Mississippi, Quitman was a champion of states' rights, was opposed to the Compromise of 1850, and urged secession unless the rights of the state were safeguarded. As an expansionist or a "Big American," as an expansionist was sometimes called, Quitman participated in the filibustering expeditions in Central America and Cuba. In a speech in Congress on April 29, 1856, he developed at length his views on the need to acquire additional territory in Mexico, Central America, and Cuba. He called attention to the continual revolutions and the state of anarchy in Mexico which tempted the European powers to seize her territory, the internal dissension in Central America which interfered with American trade and invited foreign governments to intervene, and the tyranny of the despotic government in Cuba. Quitman quoted with approval John Quincy Adams's statement that "Cuba's commanding position . . . gives it an importance . . . with which that of no other foreign territory can be compared." He called upon the federal government to secure a safe and unobstructed passage of American trade in all these areas. He also took an extreme pro-Southern stand on the right of Southerners to take their slaves into Kansas, and he demanded federal protection of slave property in the territory.

Robert J. Walker, born in Pennsylvania in 1801, was a graduate of the university of that state. He moved to Mississippi in 1826, where he became a successful lawyer, land speculator, and planter who, in his early years, was an ardent champion of slavery. In 1838 he attacked Henry Clay as an abolitionist and declared that no "man could get his vote for the presidency who had denounced me and my constituency with grievous wrongs upon the slaves." In an argument before the United States Supreme Court in 1841 he argued that the laws of Mississippi declare that "the slave shall be treated with humanity . . . the slave is secured by law kindness and proper treatment, comfortable lodging, food and clothing and proper care in infancy, sickness, and old age." In 1836 Walker was elected to the United States Senate, where he was recognized as a supporter of the rights of the states under the Constitution, but at the same time he was a champion of national sovereignty. Walker was largely responsible for the passage of the Pre-Emption Act of 1841, and he introduced and pushed through Congress a resolution recognizing the independence of Texas. He also played a prominent role in the nomination and election of James K. Polk to the presidency in 1844. Polk rewarded Walker by naming him secretary of the treasury. In this post Walker was the author of the Tariff Act of 1846, which was based on the principles of free trade, tariff for revenue only, and the warehouse system. Walker was also influential in the establishment of the Independent Treasury. An ardent expansionist, a "Big American," Walker favored the annexation of much of Mexico. He was appointed governor of the territory of Kansas by

President Buchanan and soon broke his alignment with the Southern pro-slavery interests. Walker became a strong Unionist and went to England during the Civil War to work against the Confederacy.

Few transplanted Yankees won the hearts of Mississipians as did Seargent S. Prentiss, who was born in Maine in 1808. Southerners of the pre–Civil War era were much given to oratory, and Prentiss with his mellifluous voice, matchless command of English, and charming personality, plus the fact that he had accepted wholeheartedly the Southern way of life including slavery, was extremely popular. After graduating from Bowdoin College Prentiss moved to Mississippi where he became a tutor, studied law, and entered the legal profession; according to his biography he "rose like an eagle cut loose from the cord which had bound it, till he soared above all in his profession in the State, and among the first orators of his time." At first slavery bothered Prentiss. He said, "Slavery is the great pest of this as well as all of the Southern States." But shortly thereafter he spoke of slavery as an evil but not nearly so bad as was believed in the North. "The slaves are well clothed, well fed, and kindly treated, and . . . fully as happy as their masters. . . . Their situation is much preferable to that of the free Negroes who infest the Northern cities." Prentiss opposed freedom for slaves unless they were taken back to Africa. The slave uprising in Mississippi in 1835, in which six whites and fifteen Negroes were killed, completed Prentiss's shift from opposition to the support of the institution of slavery. He declared that this incident should "serve as a warning to the abolitionist . . . of the great injury they are doing the slaves . . . by meddling with them."

Prentiss entered politics as a Whig in 1835 and was elected a member of the Mississippi legislature. In that body he worked for a convention to revise the state constitution and for railroads connecting Vicksburg with New Orleans and Nashville. He was elected to Congress in 1837, served one term only, and returned to Mississippi, where he practiced law and engaged in public speaking. He bitterly opposed the repudiation of the state debt by the Democratic legislature and, in a public address in 1841, argued that the state was constitutionally, legally, and morally bound to pay her bonds sold on account of the Union bank. Prentiss was active in the presidential campaign of 1844 and made nationalism versus the rising tide of sectionalism the major issue. He condemned those who were "stirring up sectional warfare between the North and the South, the West and the East . . . Nationalism [he said] is the highest good of the whole country, North, South, East and West." Prentiss took a very positive stand against the Wilmot Proviso. He regarded it as a violation of the consitutional rights of Southerners. But Prentiss's chief interest during his last years was the preservation of the Union. In an address in 1845 he emphasized liberty, education, democracy, and nationalism. On the last point he said: "We love the land of our adoption, so do we that of our birth. Let us be ever true to both; and always exert ourselves in maintaining our country, the integrity of the Republic. Accursed, then, be the hand put forth to loosen the golden cord of Union; thrice accursed the traitorous lips whether of Northern fanatic or Southern demagogue which shall propose its severance." In one of his last public address-es before his death in 1850, he expressed the hope that "the time would never come when a citizen of New Orleans would be a stranger in Boston nor a citizen of Boston a foreigner in New Orleans." He pointed out "the faults on *both sides,* North and South, and set forth the incalculable woes that would follow disunion." But he considered that if such a calamity should come he "would cast his lot with the land of his wife and children." The Yankee had in fact become a Southerner.

John MacPherson Berrien and Thomas Butler King may be considered as typical representatives of the Georgia Yan-kee political leaders of the middle period. Berrien was born in New Jersey in 1781 and was a graduate of Princeton University. Having studied law, he moved to Georgia and entered politics in 1810. He moved up the ladder from solicitor to judge of the superior court. He then served as a member of both houses of the state legislature and was elected to the United States Senate in 1824. In that body he opposed protective tariffs, supported wholeheartedly the right of slaveholders to carry their slaves into the newly organized territories, and was a champion of the Bank of the United States. President Andrew Jackson appointed Berrien attorney general in his cabinet in 1829 but forced his resignation in 1831, because of Berrien's position in the Peggy Eaton imbroglio. Berrien then returned to Georgia to practice law. Jackson's bold and positive action in regard to South Carolina's nullification of the tariff acts in 1833 brought a vigorous reply from Berrien in a Fourth of July address in 1834. Reviewing the evolution of the United States government from the Declaration of Independence through the Articles of Confederation to the Constitution, he concluded: "The rejection of the preceding theories force upon us the conviction that the States themselves, each for itself is the supreme arbiter. The parties to this compact[i.e., the United States Constitution] are *Sovereign States. They have designated no Common Umpire.*" He called to his support Jackson's own support of Georgia in the case of *Worcester* v. *Georgia.* Berrien returned to the United States Senate as a Whig in 1841 and served until 1852. He opposed John C. Calhoun's extreme views on Southern rights, but he did vote against the admission of California as a free state and the slave provisions of the Compromise of 1850. He took the position that the Southern states should develop industry and trade so as to become economically independent of the North. He halfheartedly supported Georgia's threat of secession in her platform of 1850. Berrien resigned his seat in the Senate in 1852. He was offered, but declined, an appointment as chief justice of the Georgia Supreme Court.

Thomas Butler King, one of five brothers who moved from Massachusetts to Georgia in 1823, had a phenomenal rise to success in business and politics, aided no doubt by his marriage to the daughter of a wealthy planter. Ten years after he settled in Georgia, King was elected to the state constitutional convention and to the state legislature as a Whig. He served in the legislature for five terms where he advocated state support for internal improvements including railroads, canals, and harbors. He was financially interested in several of the early Georgia railroads and was president of the Brunswick Railroad and Canal Company. King was elected to Congress in 1839 and served for eight years. As chairman of the Naval Affairs Committee King influenced the passage of legislation in various areas including the merchant marine, the construction of steam vessels for the navy, mail subsidies to steamship lines, and the establishment of the Naval Observatory. President Zachary Taylor sent King to California in 1849 to investigate conditons and report back in regard to statehood for California, and in 1851 he appointed King collector of customs at the port of San Francisco. When California was admitted as a free state, some Georgians accused King of having influenced such action. King published a denial in *An Address to the People* in which he said he never "received secret instructions, written or verbal, from the President of the United States, or any member of his Cabinet, on the subject of slavery . . . [nor did he] attempt to influence the people of California to decide the question of slavery one way or the other." King also pointed out that he had published a letter before the admission of California in which he had said: "I assert, unequivocally . . . that the Congress of the United States does not possess the constitutional power to abolish slavery in the District of Columbia, or in the Territories of the United States." King returned to Georgia and renewed his interests in railroad construction. He promoted the development of railroad connections from Georgia through the Gulf Coast states to Texas

and advocated aid for the construction of a road from El
Paso to the Pacific Coast. He was one of a group which
opened a line of steamers direct from Savannah, Georgia, to
Belgium in 1860. King closed his career as Georgia's commissioner to Belgium, France, and England in 1861–1862.

A large number of Yankees served as governors of the
Southern states during the first half of the nineteenth century, many of whom made significant contributions to the
South. Representative of the group was Joseph Johnson, who
was born in New York in 1785, moved to Virginia in 1801,
and was the first nonnative governor of that state. Johnson
was self-educated but widely read. He served in the state
legislature a total of nine years and Congress fourteen years
and suffered only one defeat. He was an ardent Democrat
and was the only member of the Virginia delegation who
favored Andrew Jackson over John Quincy Adams in the
presidential election of 1824. He was a member of the Virginia Constitutional Convention of 1850, was chairman of the
committee on suffrage, and successfully led the fight for man-
hood suffrage. He was elected governor of Virginia in 1852
and again in 1854, the first governor elected by popular vote
in that state. His administration was a liberal, progressive
one. Johnson submitted a program to the legislature calling
for an extensive system of canals and railroads which was
adopted by the legislature with little or no change. As a
Jacksonian Democrat Johnson had denounced nullification
in the 1830s, and he opposed secession in 1860. He hoped for
a peaceful settlement of the sectional issue. When President
Lincoln called for troops, Johnson announced that his first
allegiance was to Virginia, and he gave his full support to the
state. Meanwhile the western counties formed the state of
West Virginia, and Johnson became an exile from his own
home. After the close of the Civil War Johnson was welcomed back to West Virginia, where he died in 1877.

Representative of the numerous Yankees who served as
chief justice of the supreme court of their adopted Southern

states was Hiram Warner. Born in Massachusetts in 1802 Warner settled in Georgia in 1819. With little or no formal education, he taught school, studied law, and was elected to the state legislature when only twenty-seven years of age. As a member of the state legislature Warner introduced and secured the passage of a bill to abolish the property qualification for membership in the legislature. Warner served as a superior court judge from 1833 to 1840 and was elected chief justice of the state supreme court in 1846 and served until 1853. Elected to the state secession convention in 1860 Warner voted against the Ordinance of Secession but signed the act when passed. He was again elected chief justice of the Georgia Supreme Court in 1867 and served until 1870.

Horace Maynard is a representative of that relatively small group of Yankees who had attained success and recognition in the Old South but gave their service to the Union during the Civil War and yet retained the respect of their Southern friends after the Civil War. Born in Massachusetts in 1814, Maynard was graduated from Amherst College in 1838, moved to Tennessee, and was a professor at the University of East Tennessee from 1839 to 1841. He then studied law and practiced his profession in Knoxville until 1857 when he was elected to Congress. A Whig in politics, Maynard supported Gen. Winfield Scott for president in 1852 and John Bell in 1860. Maynard was bitterly opposed to secession, but after some of the Southern states had seceded, he spoke long and fervently in Congress and various Northern cities where he appealed for a sympathetic understanding of the Southern people in the vain hope of appeasement and unity. On February 6, 1861, he spoke in Congress on the topic "Let Us Remain One People! An Appeal to the North." In this speech he took the position that the Southern disunionists were sincere and able patriots who had been frightened by the denunciation of the Northerners who preached the "irrepressible conflict." Maynard placed a large part of the blame for secession upon the rapid increase of the spirit of antislavery, abolitionism, free soilism, the anti-Southern crusade, and the solidification of all the free states, except New Jersey, in the Republican party. Maynard charged that Northern men of all shades of opinion were "bedded together, heads and heels covered by a single blanket and that woven of African wool." In a speech in New York on February 22, 1861, he was even more vehement in his condemnation of ministers who had never been south of the Mason-Dixon Line but denounced Southern patriots as traitors and repeated the false charge that "masters sell their own flesh and blood" in their Negro offspring. When war came Maynard supported the Union and held the post of attorney general in Tennessee from 1863 to 1865. After a long political career in Congress, as minister to Turkey, and as postmaster general in President Grant's cabinet, Maynard retired to his home in Knoxville, Tennessee, where he died in 1882.

3.   The Texas Yankees

Yankees played a unique role in Texas in that they helped to establish and lead the independent Republic of Texas, and then they helped it to join the United States as the Lone Star State in 1845. This development had its beginning with Moses Austin, a Yankee born in Vermont in 1761. In 1783 Austin joined a business firm in Philadelphia which he reorganized in 1784 and established a branch, Moses Austin and Company, in Richmond, Virginia. There he engaged successfully in the Chiswell Lead Mines of that state in 1789 and moved to Missouri in 1796, where he established the town of Potosi and organized the Bank of St. Louis in 1816. His bank failed, and Austin moved to San Antonio, Texas, where he received permission from the Spanish authorities to establish a colony. Austin died before he could carry out his plans and his son, Stephen Fuller Austin, took over and became the leader in the American colonization of Texas. Conflict developed between the colony and the Mexican government, but after a short war the Texans won their independence and in

1836 established the Republic of Texas. President Andrew Jackson of the United States recognized the new government on March 3, 1837

Nine years later Texas was admitted as a state in the United States. Since Texas has a background quite different from that of the other states and territories of the Union, a separate study of the role of the Texas Yankee seems appropriate. Thumbnail sketches of representative leaders of the Republic and the state of Texas will make clear the character and quality of these Texas Yankees.

David Gouverneur Burnet, born in New Jersey in 1788, was educated in his native state and later served as an apprentice in a New York countinghouse. After a career that took him on a filibustering expedition to South America, a sojourn in Louisiana, and some years spent on the western plains with the Comanche Indians, Burnet settled in Texas in the early 1830s. He served as a judge in the municipality of Austin and as a member of a commission which attempted reconciliation with Mexico in 1835. A member of the constitutional convention of 1836, Burnet was elected by that body the first president of the Republic of Texas. He served as vice president from 1840 to 1842 and as secretary of state under President Mirabeau Buonaparte Lamar. He was ever loyal to his state and nation and bitterly opposed the secession of Texas from the Union; he took no part in the Civil War. He was elected to the United States Senate from Texas in 1866, but was not seated.

Anson Jones was born in Massachusetts in 1798, studied at Jefferson Medical College, and practiced medicine in Philadelphia from 1827 to 1832. He moved to Texas in 1833 and became active in the movement for independence from Mexico. He presided over a meeting in 1835 which drew up resolutions in favor of a declaration of independence. He was a surgeon in the Texas Army of Independence, a member of the Texas congress of 1836, Texas minister to the United States (1837–1839), member of the Texas senate and vice president of the republic (1839–1840), and secretary of state (1841–1844). He was elected president of the republic in 1844 and held that post until Texas was admitted to the Union in 1845. Jones was an ardent champion of slavery but a stong Unionist. He published an article in the Galveston *Tri-Weekly News* of March 27, 1856, in which he developed at length his views on the slavery issue. He charged that the abolitionists intended to bring about the forceful overthrow of slavery or drive the slave states from the Union. He defended the institution of slavery as perfectly consistent with the Constitution. He said, "If our government is destined to fall to pieces it will be by some foolish or wicked internal dissension, some *ism*, like abolitionism." Again he said, "We want no compromise with Abolitionism—we will submit to none. . . . It is idle to suppose that there can be a peaceful destruction of the Union, [and] I would sooner see the continent swallowed up by some great convulsion of Nature, than to see our Union broken." He was a candidate for a seat in the United States Senate in 1857. Failing election, Jones committed suicide in 1858.

Ashbel Smith, born in Connecticut in 1805, received the bachelor of arts and doctor of medicine degrees from Yale University and then studied surgery in France. He settled in Texas and in 1837 became surgeon general in the Texas army. He represented the Republic of Texas as minister to England and France (1842–1844) and was secretary of state of Texas in 1845. Smith negotiated the Smith-Cuevas Treaty by which Mexico recognized the independence of Texas. As a member of the Texas legislature in 1855 Smith sponsored common schools and internal improvements. Smith supported secession of Texas from the Union in 1861. He served as a brigadier general in the Civil War and was cited for gallantry at the battles of Shiloh and Vicksburg. After the Civil War Smith helped to organize the University of Texas. He died at his plantation in 1886.

Samuel Rhodes Fisher was born in Pennsylvania in 1794

and moved to Texas in 1830 where he became a planter and a merchant. He was representative of the Yankees who changed their opinion of slavery after moving to the slave states. He declared in 1830 that he "detested slavery," but he later advocated the admission of slaves into the Texas republic on economic grounds. Fisher wrote Stephen F. Austin that he had become "firmly persuaded that the free admission of slaves in the State of Texas . . . would tend more to the rapid introduction of respectable emigrants than any other course which could be pursued." Fisher was a member of the convention which framed the republic's constitution and later served as secretary of the navy in President Sam Houston's administration. President Houston suspended Fisher for malfeasance in office after he had gathered evidence showing that Fisher had authorized a naval attack upon Mexican coastal towns far removed from the Texas border, whereupon the Texas senate then ordered Fisher's dismissal. Fisher was murdered shortly thereafter.

Three Yankees represented Texas in the United States Congress prior to the Civil War. Volney Erskine Howard, a native of Maine, moved to Mississippi where he had a successful career as a court reporter and compiler of the statutes and reports of that state. Moving to Texas, Howard served as a member of the constitutional convention of 1845 and of the United States House of Representatives from 1849 to 1853. Timothy Pillsbury, a native of Massachusetts, served in both houses of legislature of the Republic of Texas, as judge of the probate court, and as a member of the national House of Representatives from 1846 to 1850. David Spanger Kauffman was born in Pennsylvania and was graduated from Princeton University. He moved to Texas and served in both houses of the congress of the Republic of Texas, as chargé d'affaires to the United States in 1845, and as a member of the United States House of Representatives from 1846 to 1851. None of the three representatives distinguished himself in Congress.

Hugh McLeod was born in New York in 1814 and was a graduate of West Point. He moved to Texas in 1836 where he became an advocate of internal improvements and built the first railroad in Texas. He represented Texas in the Southern Commercial Convention of 1855 where he was a strong supporter of Southern rights. When Texas seceded from the Union in 1861, McLeod offered his services to the Confederacy. As a colonel he assisted in seizing the federal gunboats on the Rio Grande and later commanded the First Texas Infantry. McLeod was killed in action in 1862.

Charles De Morse, a native of Massachusetts, moved to Texas where he became the editor of the *Northern Standard* and ardently championed slavery and Southern rights. Demanding that the Fugitive Slave Law be enforced at all costs, he said: "We had rather know that the gutters of Boston run fuller of gore than ever they did of water than of fanatics there." Again he wrote that the day on which "any attempt is made by the North to repeal or alter the Fugitive Slave Law, or the failure to carry it out, sees the beginning of the end." De Morse was also an ardent secessionist. "To remain in the Union," he said, "was not only dastardly and despicable in appearance" but would also be futile. "We should go out, we will go out. We can do well in a Southern Confederacy. [But] we shall mourn even as we approve severance as a stern necessity." De Morse entered the Confederate Army as a colonel in the cavalry in 1862. He was wounded on July 17, 1863. Promoted to brigadier general in 1864, he won a brilliant victory near Camden, Arkansas.

Elisha Marshall Pease was born in Connecticut in 1812 and moved to Texas in 1835. He was one of the ablest, most influential, and most successful of the many Yankees who settled in Texas. His rise to leadership was phenomenal and his career was a distinguished one. He served the republic as secretary of the Committee of Public Safety and as secretary of state of the provincial government, was a member of the constitutional convention and of the committee which framed the constitution and drafted the ordinances of the new republic, and he "drafted the laws creating and defining the duties of the county offices." He was chief clerk of the navy and treasury departments, secretary of the treasury, and district attorney for the republic. He served in both houses of the state legislature and was governor of Texas from 1853 to 1857. His administration was the most significant one in Texas before the Civil War. Among his notable achievements were the payment of the Texas Revolutionary War debt; the creation of a School Fund of $2 million and the setting aside of alternate sections of public lands for public schools; the establishment of an orphanage, an insane asylum, and schools for the deaf, the dumb, and the blind; and the establishment of a special fund for the support of a state university. Pease was a Unionist and opposed secession as a sure path to destruction. He remained in the state during the Civil War but took no part in public affairs. After the war ended, he joined the Republican party and was appointed provisional governor of Texas in 1867, a post he filled with distinction until he resigned in 1869. He died in 1883.

In conclusion it should be emphasized that the Yankees made significant contributions to government and politics in the Old South. They aided in the movement for independence and, according to John Adams, cast the deciding vote in that first step in the development of the United States— the first of the great democratic republics of modern times. They contributed greatly to the framing of the Constitution, especially those provisions involving the great compromise of representation and taxation. They participated in the adoption of the first state constitutions and served as the first governors of their states. They also played leading roles in the organization of the first new states, which were Kentucky and Tennessee, and later in the organization of Mississippi and Texas. They served as leaders during the period of growing tension between the North and South over slavery and territorial expansion. Quitman, King, Walker, and Slidell, leaders of the Young America Movement of the 1840s and 1850s, had visions of greatly expanding the nation, but they were hampered by the slavery issue. Livingston gained international fame as one of the greatest legal philosophers and reformers of modern times. Jones and Smith were the architects of the Republic and state of Texas. Yankees also served as chief justices of four of the Southern states. When one considers their limited number, the Yankees probably scored higher than the native Southerners.

T W O

Educational Leaders

1. State Universities

TWENTIETH-CENTURY ATHLETIC DIRECTORS AND
coaches in Southern colleges and state universities recruit
many of their better football and basketball players from
north of the Mason-Dixon Line, but it was the founders
and trustees of colleges in the Old South who went to the
North to recruit presidents and professors for their institutions. There was hardly a college in the South prior to
the Civil War that did not have a Yankee president, and
some of them had ten or more professors. In general the
quality of the Yankee teachers was high. This was true
of those in state universities, the denominational colleges,
and the many private academies scattered throughout the
South. In like manner nearly all the tutors and governesses
in the homes of the wealthy planters were New England
Yankees. Their fanatical zeal for education led "the Yankee
teachers to perform prodigies for learning in nearly every
state" in the Old South.

If the Southern colonies had done little for the advancement of education, the Southern states were pioneer leaders
in establishing state-supported universities. Georgia and
North Carolina both claim the distinction of having established the first state university, but they actually share that
honor. The Georgia legislature chartered a state university
in 1785, but it was not opened until 1801. The University of
North Carolina, chartered by the legislature in 1789, opened
its doors to students in 1795. The trustees chose for the first

39

president of the University of North Carolina Joseph Caldwell, born in New Jersey in 1773 and a 1791 graduate of
Princeton University, who had been a member of the faculty
of his alma mater. Caldwell was an able administrator and
selected an excellent and well-trained faculty. The first two
members chosen were Charles Wilson Harris and Shepard
H. Kolloch, both natives of New Jersey and alumni of
Princeton University. Two of the abler Yankee professors
recruited by President Caldwell were Denison Olmsted and
Elisha Mitchell, both of whom were natives of Connecticut
and graduates of Yale College. Olmsted had studied under
Benjamin Silliman, one of the leading scientists of the
period, and had taught at Yale University. Olmsted began
a geological survey of North Carolina, and Mitchell completed it and published the first geological survey made by
any state in the Union. Interested in the geological forma-
tion of mountains, Mitchell was the first to explore and
measure the height of what was to be called Mount Mitchell and to establish the fact that it is the highest peak in the
United States east of the Mississippi River. Incidentally,
Mitchell lost his life while on a geological tour of the
mountain named for him.

President Caldwell was interested in the well-being and
progress of the state as well as the university, and he called
on the people to move forward through a program of public improvements. While on a tour of Europe in 1824, he
purchased philosophical and scientific apparatus for laboratories, and in 1830 the university erected a building for a
telescope and other instruments which is generally regarded
as the first observatory at any American university. Caldwell's *Letters of Carlton* had considerable influence on the
development of roads and canals and won for him the title
of "Father of Internal Improvements in North Carolina."
His *Letters on Popular Education Addressed to the People,* published in 1832, called for tax-supported public elementary
and secondary education and was influential in the estab-

lishment of a state-supported public school system in 1837.
Caldwell was employed as a "scientific expert" for the party
which surveyed the North Carolina–South Carolina boundary line in 1813. He died in 1835 at the peak of his career.
One of his contemporaries wrote that North Carolina was
"indebted to . . . [Caldwell's] agency directly or indirectly
more than to any other individual for the very remarkable
change that has taken place in the . . . intellectual character
of our state in the last forty years."

The story of the organization and development of the
University of Georgia is similar to that of North Carolina
in that many of the Georgia leaders were New Englanders.
Lyman Hall, a native of Connecticut, graduate of Yale,
and signer of the Declaration of Independence for Georgia,
first suggested the idea of a state university in Georgia.
Abraham Baldwin, also a native of Connecticut and a
graduate of Yale, introduced a bill in the state legislature
and secured a charter for the University of Georgia in
1785. Baldwin was named chairman of a board of trustees and acting president of the institution until a president
and faculty could be chosen. Josiah Meigs, a native of Connecticut, a graduate of Yale and a professor of mathematics
at his alma mater, was chosen president of the University of
Georgia in 1800. Mrs. Meigs complained that they "were
exiled from their native state in the backwoods of Georgia
only twelve miles from the Cherokee Indians." Needless to
say, she was unhappy. To make matters worse Meigs became
embroiled in politics and a religious controversy between two
factions in the state. He was deposed from the presidency in
1810 and lost his professorship in 1811. The next year he took
a position as surveyor general for the United States. Henry
Kolloch, a Yale graduate, was offered the presidency of the
University of Georgia but refused it. Robert Finley, a native
of New Jersey and a graduate of Princeton University, was
then appointed but died within a year. Alonzo Church, a
native of Vermont and a graduate of Middlebury College

where he had been a member of the faculty since 1819, was appointed president of the University of Georgia in 1829 and served until 1859. He was successful in building up the faculty, despite religious discord between the various denominations. Church, however, became involved in a controversy with the Le Conte brothers, John and Joseph, who were scientists, over the modernization of the curriculum, and Church resigned. The University of Georgia, like that of North Carolina, was throughout the antebellum period almost constantly under the control of New England Yankees.

Jonathan Maxcy, a native of Massachusetts and a graduate of Brown University, was chosen the first president of the University of South Carolina in 1804, and he held the position until his death in 1820. He had been the first professor of divinity and president of Brown University for thirteen years before removing to the University of South Carolina. He was highly successful in drawing students from the "up country" as well as the "low" of South Carolina and thus helped to curb the sectionalism that had theretofore divided the state. He built up a strong faculty and won national recognition for the university. A contemporary voiced the view that "he had guided the University with such energy, ability and foresight that the entire state was his debtor."

Maxcy's successor at the University of South Carolina was the controversial publicist and scientist Dr. Thomas Cooper. Born in England, Cooper had been in the United States since 1794, long enough to qualify as a Yankee. A controversial figure, Cooper was tried, convicted, and fined under the Alien and Sedition Law in 1800. He had been professor of chemistry at Dickinson College from 1811 to 1815 and of chemistry and mineralogy at the University of Pennsylvania from 1816 to 1819. Thomas Jefferson hoped to secure Cooper as a professor at the University of Virginia, but the Virginians would not accept such a radical thinker. Cooper was appointed professor of chemistry at the University of South Carolina in 1820 and served as President of that institution from 1821 to 1835. He was influential in establishing the first medical school and the first insane asylum in South Carolina. Cooper was a bitter opponent of protective tariffs and strong central government; a foe of tyranny and yet a defender of slavery, he repudiated much of Jefferson's social philosophy. He calculated the value of the Union and favored nullification of the tariff acts of 1828 and 1832. Despite his general accord in political philosophy with the majority of South Carolinians, Cooper was finally eased out of the presidency of the university because of his lack of religious orthodoxy. He spent his last years in editing *The Statutes At Large of South Carolina* in five volumes. Cooper was a significant figure in his war on tyranny and is entitled to a conspicuous place in the history of intellectual liberty and free speech.

Charles F. McCoy, a native of Pennsylvania who had been a member of the University of Georgia faculty for a number of years, was chosen president of the University of South Carolina in 1851. His tenure as president was for two years only, and he made no significant contribution to the university. He did, however, devise a mutual mortality insurance plan which the legislature adopted for the state.

The University of Alabama had its origin in an act of Congress, passed April 20, 1818, which set aside an entire section of public land in the Alabama territory for a "Seminary of Learning." The legislature of Alabama in 1820 accepted the land grant and changed the name of the institution to the University of Alabama. On April 12, 1831, the university was opened at Tuscaloosa with Dr. Alva Woods of Vermont as president and Dr. Gordon Saltonstall of New York as professor. Woods had a distinguished career behind him. He had been graduated from Harvard College, studied theology at Andover Theological Seminary, served on the faculty of Columbian College in Washington, D.C., and served as president of Transylvania University in Kentucky from 1828 to 1831. Saltonstall held a bachelor of arts

degree from Union College and a doctor of medicine degree
from the New York College of Physicians and Surgeons.
President Woods was never happy in Tuscaloosa: he had
lived too long in the city with greater cultural opportunities
than the Alabama village offered. He could not get along
with his faculty and found the students obstreperous and
difficult to discipline; furthermore, his open and bitter opposition to slavery aroused and alienated the people of the state
and of the college community. He resigned the presidency in
1837 and left the state. Saltonstall found the students so
poorly prepared and lacking in mental discipline that he
resigned his professorship after two years. Other Yankees
who were to join the Alabama University faculty before the
Civil War were Michael Tuomey, John Williams Mallet,
Caleb Huse, and Frederick A. P. Barnard.

Tuomey, trained in geology at Rensselaer Polytechnic Institute, did some teaching but was engaged primarily in
geological surveys of the state. His *Geological Report,* the first
for the state, was for its time thorough and accurate. Tuomey
is credited with the first exact atomic weight ever made in
America. His report on the finding of the atomic weight of
lithium was published in the *American Journal of Science* in
1856. Mallet, with a degree from the University of Dublin
and a doctorate from the University of Göttingen, had been
a professor of chemistry at Amherst College before moving
to Alabama. He worked with Tuomey on the state geological
survey and completed and edited a second *Geological Report.*
Mallet joined the Confederate Army in 1861, became superintendent of the laboratories of the Confederate states, and
had a distinguished career under Gen. Josiah Gorgas, a
Pennsylvania Yankee, who was to become president of the
University of Alabama after the Civil War.

Caleb Huse, Massachusetts born and a graduate of West
Point, was, upon the recommendation of the superintendent
of West Point, appointed superintendent of cadets at the
University of Alabama. As a Yankee he was at first very

unpopular, and the students threatened to run him out of town. Huse offered his resignation, but President Landon C. Cabell, a native of Virginia, refused to accept it. Huse then took the cadet corps to Montgomery, the state capital, where the legislature was discussing the burning issue of secession. The cadets were warmly received, and Huse soon became very popular with them. When secession came, Huse offered his services to the Confederacy, and the cadet body did likewise. Huse served the Confederacy with distinction.

Frederick A. P. Barnard, a native of Massachusetts and a graduate of Yale University, was by far the most distinguished person connected with the University of Alabama prior to 1860. He was professor of mathematics and chemistry from 1838 to 1854. Before going to Alabama Barnard had taught in the American Institute for the Deaf and Dumb in Hartford, Connecticut, and the New York Institution for the Deaf and Dumb. A brilliant scholar and a stimulating teacher at the University of Alabama, Barnard was popular with the students, but unpopular with the president of the university because of his addiction to strong drink. Barnard reformed and became a priest in the Episcopal church and found time to edit a newspaper, the *Monitor* and to write poetry for the *Southern Magazine.* Barnard served on a United State commission that surveyed the boundary line between Florida and Alabama, wrote the commission's report, and was instrumental in establishing an astronomical observatory at the University of Alabama. He developed a method for producing stereopticon plates for binocular vision with single exposure and was the first to use chlorine to speed up the luminous impressions of the daguerreotype in photography. Barnard became a nationally known scholar and was one of the founders and served as president of the American Association for the Advancement of Science. He was also a member of the National Academy of Science. He was the author of *History of the United States Coast Survey* and *Recent Progress in Science.* Barnard resigned his position at the University of

Alabama in 1854 to take a position at the University of Mississippi. One writer described Barnard while at Alabama as "a marvel of intellectual brilliance and practical versatility." Barnard himself wrote late in his life that "some of the happiest and most fruitful years of my life" were spent at the University of Alabama.

Barnard's early years at the University of Mississippi were fruitful and satisfying. He had the complete support of President Augustus Baldwin Longstreet and was given a free hand to carry on his scientific work. He made a study of the state's seminary fund and found the state legislature in arrears to the university. Longstreet submitted Barnard's finding to the legislature which, after a study of the problem, increased the payment to the university, by what was in that period, a handsome figure for the university. Barnard was elected president of the University of Mississippi in 1856. In that office he emphasized sciences and general education and organized a graduate master of arts program. He appealed successfully to the legislature for greater financial support and secured funds for a library, an observatory, and laboratories for the sciences. He also stressed the need for a study of agriculture. In doing so he repeated arguments he had used in a Fourth of July oration in 1851 when he had advocated diversification of agriculture and development of the textile industry and manufactures of all sorts in order to bring the state increased revenue for schools, libraries, and lecture halls.

Barnard's position on the slavery issue was clear-cut. He held that the United States Constitution guaranteed slavery and that the government was obligated to protect slave property. In 1860 he declared: "I am a slave holder, and, if I know myself I am sound on the slave question." But he became embroiled in a bitter controversy over the rape of one of his Negro slave girls by a university student. Barnard proposed to dismiss the student. After a hearing, a faculty committee voted five to three that "although the Faculty are morally convinced of . . . [the student's] guilt, yet they do not consider the evidence adduced to substantiate the charges as sufficient, legally, to convict him." The student, however, left the university. Public sentiment was hostile to Barnard, but the board of trustees took the testimony of every member of the faculty and voted unanimously that Barnard "stands fully and favorably acquitted of every charge brought against him. We have confidence in his ability and integrity, and his fitness for the position is increased rather than diminished, and declare our full conviction that his labors are doing great service to the cause of education and science and placing the University upon an immovable base." Barnard submitted his resignation but the board refused to accept it, and he remained in his office for some time after the students had left the university at the outbreak of the Civil War. The board of trustees gave Barnard an honorary degree of doctor of sacred theology and cited him as a man "whose reputation as a practical educator entitles him preeminently to a notice · in these pages and who, as a writer on subjects connected with collegiate education, stands second to no other in the country." The board now accepted Barnard's resignation, but immediately gave him an assignment to visit colleges in the South from Mississippi to Virginia and report back to the board.

In Richmond, Barnard consulted with Confederate officials and left the Confederacy in May of 1862. He published a pamphlet *A Letter to the President of the United States,* in which he expressed his feelings toward the Old South. He said: The rebellion "found me in the possession of a highly honorable position, in the bosom of a delightful social circle, . . . charged with the care of a great educational institution, . . . around me a band of young men numbering some hundreds, whom, for every magnanimous and generous quality, and of whose devoted attachment to myself I had the most convincing reason to be assured. . . . [I was] sustained and cheered in the discharge of a difficult responsibility and duty, by the encouraging voice of a wide circle of influential friends."

Yankees also played a leading roll in the establishment and development of the University of Tennessee. In 1794 Samuel Carrick, a native of Pennsylvania, was elected president of Blount College in Tennessee, and he continued in this post when the name was changed to East Tennessee College in 1808. David A. Sherman, a New Englander, succeeded Carrick and was in turn followed in 1835 by Joseph Estabrook, a native of New Hampshire and a graduate of Dartmouth College. The college, raised to university status by state action, was renamed East Tennessee University in 1840, and Estabrook continued as president until 1850. He sanctioned slavery and was highly popular with university students and the people of the region. His antics also titillated their sense of humor. He "was given to elegant ruffles and fine boots, to prodigious use of snuff, to shooting on Fast Day, and capping all to dream dreams which told him . . . how to win a $5,000 lottery." George Cooke, a native of New Hampshire and a graduate of Dartmouth College, followed Estabrook as president of East Tennessee University. He was critical of slavery and championed a member of his faculty who was known as one of the most ardent abolitionists in the community. Cooke resigned under pressure in 1857, but the university had been controlled by New England Yankees throughout most of the period from 1794 to 1860.

Among the Yankees who were leaders in the early development of Missouri were John Hiram Lathrop and George Clinton Swallow. Lathrop, the first president of the University of Missouri, was a native of New York and a graduate of Yale University. He had studied law but chose the teaching profession as a career and taught mathematics, natural philosophy, and political economy at Hamilton College in New York. As president of the University of Missouri from 1841 to 1849, he was able to attract a young and well-trained faculty. But in the late 1840s the controversy over slavery and sectionalism became so bitter that he resigned and went to the University of Wisconsin as chancellor. He returned to Missouri as professor of English and political philosophy in 1859 and ended his career as president of the university in 1866. Swallow, a native of Maine and a graduate of Bowdoin College, was a professor of chemistry and geography at the University of Missouri in 1850. He was influential in establishing an agricultural and mechanical association in 1852 and a separate Department of Agriculture at the university in 1858. He served as state geologist from 1853 to 1860 and published his first report in 1855. He ended his career as dean of the College of Agriculture.

The establishment of a state university in Louisiana came too late to exert any major influence on the educational life of the South prior to 1860. But the legislature did provide in 1859 for the establishment of the Louisiana State Scientific Literary and Military Academy, later to be known as Louisiana State University. The trustees appointed as superintendent of the academy one William Tecumseh Sherman who made significant contributions to the Old South, some of which are still with us.

Thomas Jefferson, father of the University of Virginia, sought faculty scholars in Europe rather than in the United States. But William Holmes McGuffey, a native of Pennsylvania and a college president, was appointed a professor at the University of Virginia in 1845, a position he held until his death in 1873. McGuffey was nationally known as the author of spelling books and readers. Most important of his works were the Eclectic Readers series in six stages or grades. Numbers five and six were published after he became a professor at the University of Virginia. The speller and readers were widely used and had great influence throughout the United States. It is estimated that more than one hundred million copies of the McGuffey readers were sold in the United States.

2. Independent and Church-related Colleges

Yankee leadership in the establishment and development of independent and church-related colleges in the Old South was much more widespread and effective in meeting the needs of the people than it was in the state universities. From Delaware in the Northeast to Texas in the Southwest and from Florida in the Southeast to Missouri in the Northwest, there was hardly an academy or college that was not sponsored by a Yankee who came to the South, as one of their number said, "for the purpose of improving education." By far the greater number of colleges were established in the Southeastern states of Maryland, Virginia, North Carolina, South Carolina, Georgia, and Alabama and in the Mississippi Valley states of Kentucky, Tennessee, and Missouri. The other Southern states had relatively few institutions of higher learning. Arkansas had none, and Florida had only one college before the Civil War. The pre–Civil War Southern colleges still in existence number about seventy-five, but they have absorbed numerous lesser institutions that were in existence before the Civil War. Short sketches of representative colleges of this group will make clear the character and contributions of the Yankee to this phase of Southern education.

Transylvania University in Lexington, Kentucky, a private institution closely allied with the Christian church, became, under the leadership of President Horace Holley in the decade from 1817 to 1827, one of the outstanding educational institutions in the United States with its schools of law and medicine, in addition to the College of Arts and Sciences. Holley, a native of Connecticut, was graduated from Yale with highest honors. During his presidency Transylvania's enrollment reached 418 students while Yale had only 319 and Harvard 286. Holley also built up the library until it was equal to the best in the nation. Edward Everett, in a letter to Sir Walter Scott, described Holley as "a philosopher, a scholar and a gentleman who has no superior in America." Holley brought to Transylvania some of the leading scholars in America. Among them was Dr. Benjamin Winslow Dudley of Pennsylvania who held a doctor of medicine degree from the University of Pennsylvania and three years of study in Europe. He performed the first successful cataract operation in the West and won international recognition for his work.

William Gibbs Hunt, a native of Boston with a degree from Harvard, went to Transylvania where he took a degree in law in 1822. He became a distinguished publisher and editor. The *Western Monitor* of Lexington, Kentucky, edited by Hunt, was one of the most important newspapers of the state, and his *Western Review . . . A Monthly Publication Devoted to Literature and Science* was widely read.

Other distinguished Yankee scholars who served Transylvania included Henry Bidleman Bascom who was president of the college from 1841 to 1849. A member of the convention of the Methodist Episcopal church in 1845, he supported the proslavery faction and joined the Methodist Episcopal church, South, of which he became a bishop. He published *Methodism and Slavery* in which he defended the institution of slavery. Thomas Winthrop Coit, a native of Connecticut and a graduate of Yale, was president of Transylvania from 1834 to 1837. Dr. Samuel Annan, a native of Pennsylvania who held a doctor of medicine degree from the University of Edinburgh, was a professor at Transylvania from 1846 to 1853, and superintendent of the state insane asylum from 1853 to 1861.

Hampden-Sydney, a small Presbyterian college in Virginia, was noted for its faculty, which was recruited largely from the Northern states. Samuel Stanhope Smith, a native of Pennsylvania and a graduate of Princeton University, was president of the college from 1776 to 1779. Smith was succeeded in the presidency by John Blair Smith, also a native of Pennsylvania and a graduate of Princeton, who was president of the college from 1779 to 1789. Smith had for some years been a teacher in a Virginia academy. An ardent patriot and supporter of the American Revolution, he organized the students into a company which he commanded in the Revolution until 1778. Deeply religious, Smith resigned the presidency and was a leader in the revival movement in Virginia in the 1790s. He was an ordained minister and was president of the Presbyterian General Assembly of 1798.

Two other Yankees, Jonathan Peter Cushing of New Hampshire and William Carroll of Pennsylvania, both graduates of Princeton, served successively as president of Hampden-Sydney from 1820 to 1838. The roster of the faculty of Hampden-Sydney prior to 1860 includes twenty-five Yankee presidents and professors who were found worthy of inclusion in the biographical dictionary *Who Was Who.*

The University of Nashville, earlier known as Cumberland University, was one of the leading educational institutions in the Old South and was widely known throughout the nation. Its reputation and fame were largely due to the leadership of Philip Lindsley, his son John Berrien, and the faculty whom they employed. Philip Lindsley was born in New Jersey in 1786 and was graduated from Princeton University in 1804. He was a member of the faculty at Princeton from 1807 to 1817 and was president from 1817 to 1823. He was so well and favorably known as an educator that he was offered, but he declined, the presidency of Transylvania and Ohio universities and Dickinson College. He accepted the presidency of the University of Nashville in 1825 and held that post until 1850. The University of Alabama and the University of Pennsylvania tried in vain to lure him away from Nashville.

In his first public address in Nashville Lindsley announced his goals for the university. He proposed that instruction be given in "all the sciences, and in every department of philosophy and literature." He looked forward to the day when the university would have "an array of able professors, libraries, cabinets of natural history, botanical gardens, astronomical observatories and chemical laboratories" equal to those of the best universities. Nor would he neglect political science, ancient and modern languages, literature, and history. In an address to faculty and students he proposed to make provision for instruction in the scientific, literary, and professional fields and also in agriculture, horticulture, civil engineering, and liberal and mechanical arts. He expressed the view that a college should encourage investigation and research, accuracy in thought, and logical discrimination. He urged students "to question the why and wherefore in all things." Lindsley established schools of law and medicine in the university which drew students from a wide area. The university could boast in 1850 that its graduates held positions as professors in many of the better academies and colleges and served in some ten state legislatures, in both houses of the United States Congress, in foreign courts, and in several editorial chairs.

Lindsley spoke out against slavery, saying, "None but the ignorant can be retained long in bondage. Let the light of science . . . shine upon the slave, wherever he is to be found in large numbers, and he will sunder his chains, and assume that attitude which the conscious dignity of his nature claims as an inherent and indefensible right." This led the *Nashville Whig* to observe: "The disposition which is too general among the people of the South and West to keep alive a feeling of aversion, a spirit of hostility, toward our fellow citizens of the North, included under the general term of Yankees, is as much to be regretted as any other evil which now prevail. . . . It originates in and is kept alive by prejudice." The prejudice to which the writer referred was the issue of slavery and abolition. Evidently Lindsley won the people of Nashville, for in 1856 a physician in the city wrote: "The great Lindsley . . . in making the seat of learning immortal left the impress of . . . [his] own mighty intellect upon . . . [his] generation and coming posterity will feel and respond to its awakening influence."

John Berrien Lindsley, physician and educator, was born in Princeton, New Jersey, in 1822. He was a graduate of the University of Nashville and received his doctor of medicine degree from the University of Pennsylvania. He became a professor in the School of Medicine at Nashville University and later dean of the school and chancellor of the university. He also organized the Tennessee College of Pharmacy. He was one of the founders of the American Association for the Advancement of Science and was a member of the American Medical Association. He organized the School of Medicine at Nashville University in 1851 and built it into one of the best-known, as well as one of the largest, medical schools in the United States. Unlike his father, John Berrien Lindsley sympathized with the South in the sectional controversy and upheld slavery, but he opposed secession. During the Civil War he was appointed post surgeon of all Confederate hospitals in Nashville, where he supervised the care of the sick and wounded, first of Confederate, and later of federal troops.

The University of Nashville did not survive the Civil War and Lindsley turned his efforts to build a public school system for Nashville. He served as superintendent of schools from 1865 to 1875. He prepared a bill which, when passed by the state legislature, created the first state board of education in Tennessee.

The impetus for Oglethorpe, the first church-related university in Georgia, came from a group of Yankees, members of the Presbyterian church, who settled in Georgia in the first quarter of the nineteenth century. A number of the group were college graduates, several of whom were teachers and preachers. Among the leaders of this group were Nathan S. S. Beman, a native of New York and a graduate of Middlebury College; Robert Finley, a native of New Jersey and a graduate of Princeton University; and Alonzo Church and Remembrance Chamberlain, both natives of Vermont and graduates of Middlebury College. Recognizing the need of education for their children, members of the two Presbyteries organized the Georgia Educational Society, which established three manual labor schools, and in 1835 they secured a charter from the state legislature and established Oglethorpe University. Carlisle Pollock Beman, a native of New York, was chosen president of the university, and Charles Wallace Howard and Samuel K. Talmage, both Yankees, were chosen members of the faculty. Beman resigned in 1840 to go back to teaching in an academy and Talmage succeeded to the presidency in 1841 and held the post until 1865. He added Dr. James Woodrow, a graduate of the University of Pennsylvania who in 1856 won a doctor of philosophy degree at the University of Heidelberg, to the faculty. Woodrow was the first professor in any college in Georgia to have an earned doctorate. He later joined the faculty of the Columbia Presbyterian Seminary. He enlisted in the Confederate Army and served as chief of the Confederate Chemical Laboratory in Columbia, South Carolina, until it was destroyed by Gen. Willian Tecumseh Sherman in 1865. Woodrow returned to his position at the seminary after the war and became involved in the controversy over evolution which grew out of Darwin's origin of species theory. While teaching at Oglethorpe before the war, Dr. Woodrow had, according to one of his students, a "sore time in teaching geology on account of Adam's biography." Woodrow took the position that the "Bible and nature are both from God. They cannot be contradictory. Apparent conflicts arise from misinterpretations of one, or the other, or both. Remove these conflicts by ascertaining and interpreting correctly the facts of both." In 1884 he published an address, *Evolution*, in which he accepted the Darwinian theory of evolution and declared that the "Bible does not teach Science; and to take its language in a scientific sense is grossly to pervert its meaning." The General Assembly of the Presbyterian church tried and condemned him as a heretic. But Woodrow was and still remains a major figure in the long struggle for freedom of speech and thought in the United States.

Three Yankees, James Huckins of New Hampshire, William M. Tryon of New York, and Horace Clark of Massachusetts, were influential in the establishment of Baylor, a Baptist university in Texas. Huckins was sent to Texas in 1839 by the Baptist Home Mission Society. Tryon moved to Georgia where he attended Mercer University and then went to Texas where he joined Huckins. Tryon pointed out the need for a Baptist college in Texas. Huckins accepted the idea and appealed to Judge Robert E. B. Baylor for financial support. Baylor agreed to finance such a program, and Tryon and Huckins secured a charter for Baylor University in 1845. Tryon was one of the organizers of the Texas Baptist Society and its secretary for a number of years. Horace Clark of Massachusetts removed to Illinois where he graduated from Shurtleff College. He then moved to Texas where he served as president of the woman's branch of Baylor University at Independence, Texas, from 1851 to 1871. One Texas historian has said that Clark did more for woman's education in Texas than any other person in the state. One other Yankee enters the early picture of Baylor. Frances Trask, a native of Massachusetts, moved to Texas in 1834 and established the Independence Female Academy in 1837, the first school chartered by the Texas republic. This school was taken over by the woman's division of Baylor University in 1845.

Milo Parker Jewett, a native of Vermont and a graduate of Dartmouth, was the founder and first president of Judson Female College in Alabama from 1835 to 1855. Under his leadership the college gained a wide reputation and attracted students from several neighboring states. Jewett became nationally known for his work and was called to New York in 1855 to formulate plans for Vassar College, of which he became the first president. Samuel S. Sherman, a native of Vermont, was president of Howard (now Samford University), the Alabama Baptist college for men, from its beginning in 1842 until 1852. Robert Paine, a native of Connecticut and a graduate of Yale, was the first president of Lagrange College in Alabama. Richard Furman, a self-educated New Yorker, moved to South Carolina where he became an outstanding Baptist leader. He developed a plan for the incorporation of the Charleston Baptist Association, was president of the first South Carolina Baptist Convention, and recommended to the Baptists that they establish a university in Washington, D.C., and feeder schools in the various states. His plan was partially carried out with the establishment of the Columbian College in Washington, Richmond University in Virginia, Furman in South Carolina, and Mercer in Georgia.

The story of the establishment and development of colleges in the Old South shows that most of them were founded through the initiative and drive of Yankees who saw the need for education ranging from the academy through the college to the university. An examination of the contemporary sources of these institutions shows that a majority of both presidents and faculty were Yankees and that they played a major role in the development of education in the South prior to 1860.

3. The Academy

Since the Old South had very few public high schools, training and preparation for college in the South was generally acquired in the academies, some public, some private, some open only to boys, some only to girls, and some few coeducational. Among the hundreds of academies which were established a large number evolved into colleges. For example, St. Johns College in Maryland grew out of King Williams School, and Washington and Lee University had its origin in the Augusta Academy. Many of the teachers in the Southern academies were Yankees, and in most of the girls' academies some, if not all, of the teachers were women. As might be expected, many of the more successful academy teachers became college professors. Short sketches of a few of the academy teachers will suffice to show the quality of their work and the significance of the academies and their teachers in the educational life of the Old South.

Abner Johnson Leavenworth, a native of Connecticut and a graduate of Amherst College, became a Congregational minister and served as chaplain of the Young Ladies Seminary in North Carolina. He then moved to Virginia where he established a Collegiate Seminary for Young Ladies. In addition to his teaching duties he became corresponding secretary of the Virginia Educational Foundation, of which he was a founder.

Franceway Ronna Cossitt, a native of New Hampshire and a graduate of Middlebury College, moved to North Carolina where he taught for some years in Vine Hill Academy, moved on to Tennessee and taught in a private academy, and thence to the Elkton Academy in Kentucky. Whether this peripatetic teacher was a good or bad one, he was influential in founding Cumberland College in Tennessee, of which he was the first president. An ardent champion of and worker for peace, he founded and edited the *Banner of Peace* from 1841 to 1849.

Emily Pillsbury Burke, a New England girl, removed to Georgia where she was a tutor in a private family and a teacher in a girls' academy. She gives an interesting picture of life in Georgia in the 1830s and 1840s in her *Reminiscences of Georgia*. She later became lady principal of Oberlin, the first coeducational college in the United States. Her career there was short and tragic. She kissed one of the men students in the hall way. He "rushed post haste to the Ladies Board and told them of the affront to his manly purity." The ladies board dismissed her, much to the disgust of the male members of the board.

Andrew L. O'Brien, a native of Pennsylvania, moved to Georgia where he taught in various academies and established three new ones, all of which according to his diary were successful. He reports that in Fort Valley he met a teacher, a "Mr. Wise, a Yankee wise by nature and by name who was my predecessor, . . . much liked by most of the Valley people."

Norman Pinney, a native of Connecticut and a graduate of Yale University, moved to Mobile, Alabama, where he was rector of Christ Church for some years. But his chief interest was his position as headmaster of the Mobile Institute for Boys from 1836 to 1862. In addition to his teaching he wrote French textbooks which were widely used in colleges as well as in academies.

The best-known and most influential Yankee teacher in any Southern academy prior to 1860 was Almira Hart Lincoln Phelps who was head of the Patapsco Female Institute in Ellicott City, Maryland, in the 1840s and 1850s. Born in Berlin, Connecticut, in 1793, Mrs. Phelps was educated at home and at the Pittsfield, Massachusetts, Seminary. Later she was permitted to attend lectures on botany, chemistry, and geology under the distinguished scientist, Prof. Amos Eaton of Rensselaer Polytechnic Institute at Troy, New York. After the death of her first husband Simeon Lincoln, Mrs. Phelps taught in various girls' schools, including the Troy, New York, Female Seminary and the West Chester, Pennsylvania, Young Ladies Seminary, both of which she served as principal.

In 1841 Mrs. Phelps became principal of the Patapsco Female Institute in Ellicott City, Maryland, where she tested the worth of her theories and carried on what one modern educational leader called the best program of women's education prior to 1860. Her students came from all sections of the country, but chiefly from Maryland and other Southern states. Under her leadership this school came to be recognized as one of the best, if not the best, school for girls in the nation. One Pennsylvania journalist wrote that Mrs. Phelps was "favorably known to the literary and scientific world" and that she had "earned a reputation in the various branches of natural science to which few of her sex can aspire." Mrs.

Phelps aimed to give a broad training in the various sciences and made that area of learning equal in importance to language and literature. In fact, she herself taught and emphasized the sciences almost to the exclusion of other subjects. Her textbook *Botany for Beginners,* according to her biographer, caused a "revolution in the progress of botanical knowledge. It taught teachers how to teach, while it led the student . . . to the interpretation and understanding of the vegetable kingdom." All of her textbooks were excellent except her *Geology* in which she attempted to reconcile science with the biblical story of creation.

Patapsco Institute included in its course of study a normal program in which the students were given instruction in pedagogical practices in classrooms. This teacher training program made Patapsco, said one writer, "a dependable source of teachers; and schools in all parts of the United States appealed to it for teachers." In addition to her texts on geology, chemistry, botany, and natural philosophy, Mrs. Phelps wrote a United States history text. In all she published nearly a score of books, some of which went through numerous printings. Her work as teacher and author influenced education in many ways—in teacher training, physical education, curriculum, and women's careers. A contemporary writer declared that Mrs. Phelps's "literary and scientific character, as well as her ability to manage and preside over such an institution [as Patapsco] have been fully sustained." Further, he said that education at Patapsco in all its branches was as good as that at Wesleyan College in Georgia, Judson College in Alabama, or Mount Holyoke in Massachusetts, and much stronger than either in mathematics and science.

In many cases the position of a teacher in an academy was a stepping-stone to a college professorship or presidency, and the number who took advantage of the opportunity was large. For example, Alonzo Church was a teacher and the headmaster at the Eatonton, Georgia, academy before he went to the University of Georgia as a professor and later became president. George Cooke was teaching in a female academy when he was chosen president of the University of East Tennessee. But evidence that teaching in an academy was a satisfying experience is illustrated in the case of Norman Pinney who taught in the Mobile, Alabama, Institute for Boys for twenty-six years. Nathan S. S. Beman, a native of Vermont, refused the presidency of the University of Georgia in order to continue teaching in the Mt. Zion Academy, and his brother, Carlisle P. Beman, resigned from the presidency of Oglethorpe University after two years to return to a teaching position in an academy.

Yankee merchants were primarily responsible for the establishment of the public schools in New Orleans. Four of the six members of a committee appointed to organize the system were New Englanders. They consulted Horace Mann in regard to the educational program and asked for suggestions for a principal and teachers. They chose John A. Shaw of Massachusetts who had been recommended by Mann as the principal. The appointment led Mann to observe: "Not only was the principal taken from Massachusetts, but also the textbooks and apparatus for the schools, all the school furniture, even the chairs for seating the scholars." He might truthfully have added teachers to the list, for twenty-four of the forty-nine teachers appointed were Yankees.

Benjamin M. Norman's evaluation of the contributions of the Yankee to the development of education in New Orleans was just as true when applied to the development of education throughout the South. He praised the "enterprising calculating hardy Yankees. They are . . . active . . . fearless, shrewd, independent, and self sufficient, and often aspiring and ambitious." They "have strict moral principles" and New Orleans "is indebted for many of those vast improvements which, as if by magic, have risen." Certainly the Yankees did much for education in the South through their leadership in establishing academies, colleges, and universi-

ties, and in supplying a large percentage of the teachers and
administrators of those institutions.

4. *Medical and Physical Scientists*

The Old South owed much of its development in medical
and physical sciences to Northern Yankees who migrated to
the South. The medical colleges of the New England and the
Middle Atlantic states sent a large number of their graduates
to the Southern states. Some twenty-five physicians moved
from the New England states to Savannah, Georgia, between
1804 and 1820. One of them, Lemuel Kolloch of Massachusetts, was the founder of Georgia's first medical society, and
numerous medical colleges were established in the South by
Yankee physicians. George Eccles, a native of Massachusetts
and a graduate of Harvard College, was the founder of the
Medical College of Louisiana. William Carr Lane, a Pennsylvania Yankee who was trained at the Pennsylvania Medical College, served as a surgeon in the Creek War from 1813
to 1816, and settled in St. Louis, Missouri, in 1823. He
founded the Missouri Medical College in 1840 and served as
professor of obstetrics in that institution. He then moved to
New Mexico territory where he served as governor for one
term. Lane later returned to St. Louis where he was a prac-
ticing physician until his death in 1863.

Samuel David Gross, one of the most distinguished physicians and surgeons of his generation, was a native of Pennsylvania with a doctor of medicine degree from Jefferson
Medical College. As professor of surgery at the Louisville
(Kentucky) Medical College he invented numerous surgical
instruments and published textbooks that were widely used
in medical colleges of the nation. He also published a full
report on Dr. Ephraim McDowell's ovariotomy in which he
gave full recognition to that pioneer Virginia surgeon for
being the first to perform such an operation. Gross's study on
internal medicine and surgery involving the nature and the
treatment of wounds of the internal organs of the body "was

at once accepted as an authority upon the subjects which it treated; and his *Treatise on Foreign Bodies in the Air Passages* was the first attempt by a physician to systematize knowledge and was a pioneer work in that field." Dr. Morell Mackinzie, a leading authority on the subject in England wrote: "This invaluable essay gives full reports on two hundred cases and is so complete that it is doubtful whether it will ever be improved upon." Gross's *Manual of Military Surgery*, published in 1861, was not available to the Confederate Army, but C. H. Wynne of Richmond, Virginia, reprinted the book from the *Southern Medical Journal* and the reprint was widely used in Confederate hospitals.

Daniel Drake was born in New Jersey in 1785 but moved with his parents to Kentucky as a small boy. He studied medicine with Dr. William Goforth and later received his medical degree at the University of Pennsylvania. Drake was a professor and dean of the Medical Department of Transylvania University from 1817 to 1827 and at the Louisville Medical Institute from 1840 to 1849. He was widely known for his *Systematic Treatise, Historical Etiological and Practical, on the Principal Diseases of the Interior Valley of North America*. Drake advocated schools for the blind and was influential in the establishment of a school for the blind in Louisville, Kentucky. Drake has been called the "most eminent early nineteenth century physician in the Central West," and "the most widely known and respected physician in the United States."

Horace H. Hayden was born in Windsor, Connecticut, in 1769 but moved to New York City at an early age. He studied dentistry and began the practice of his profession in 1792. Hayden moved to Baltimore in 1800 where he continued his profession, studied medicine, and was licensed as a physician by the medical faculty of Baltimore in 1810. He served as a surgeon in the War of 1812. Hayden's major interest, however, was dentistry, and he taught dentistry at night and gave lectures on dental physiology and pathology

to students of the University of Maryland. Hayden was the
prime mover for a dental school, and in 1839 he petitioned
the state legislature to establish a dental college. That body
granted a charter in 1840 for the Baltimore College of Dental Surgery, the first such school in America. Hayden was
chosen president of the college but also taught courses in
dental sciences. He was awarded a doctor of dental surgery
degree and was given an honorary doctor of medicine degree
by the University of Maryland. Hayden was also the leader
in the organization and establishment of the American Society of Dental Surgery and the founder of the American
Dental College. For many years the graduates of Hayden's
dental college dominated the profession in America. In 1860
some 63 percent of the students in the dental college were
natives of the Southern states, while 30 percent came from
the Northern states and 7 percent from foreign countries. In
the *Dictionary of American Biography* Hayden is described as
"one of the foremost dentists of his time, and he lived to see
the realization of his most cherished project, the establishment of dentistry as an organized profession."

John Leonard Riddell, physician, scientist, and inventor,
was born in Massachusetts in 1807 and educated at the
Rensselaer Polytechnic Institute in New York and the Cincinnati Medical College. Riddell was professor of chemistry
at the Medical College of Louisiana from 1836 until his
death in 1865. Among Riddell's published works was *Louisiana Plants* in which he reported new species. It was widely and
favorably received. Riddell served on a commission in 1844
to devise means for protecting New Orleans from the over-
flow of the Mississippi River. He did research in and discovered the microscopic characteristics of the blood and black
vomit in yellow fever. He was commissioned in 1853 to study
and inquire into the origin, causes, and character of yellow
fever epidemics. In 1851 Riddell devised a binocular microscope for dividing light from single objectives. He demonstrated   the   microscope   before   the   New   Orleans

Physico-Medico Society in 1852 and displayed it before the American Association for the Advancement of Science. Although some scoffed at his inventions, Riddell won wide recognition for his development and contribution to the use of the microscope. He was one of the organizers of the Louisiana State Medical Society, and in addition to his active career as a professor in the state medical college he found time to serve as the official melter and refiner in the United States Branch Mint in New Orleans from 1838 to 1849.

William Barton Rogers, a native of Pennsylvania, was educated at the College of William and Mary, where his father was professor of chemistry and natural history. He taught school in Baltimore, Maryland, where he promoted a plan for a technical high school and later drew a plan for a polytechnic college in Virginia. Rogers succeeded his father in the chair of chemistry in William and Mary and later moved to the University of Virginia, where he held the chair of chemistry and physical geography. His work in the latter field led to a study of mountain ranges that brought national recognition and won for him membership in the American Philosophical Society, the presidency of the American Association for the Advancement of Science, and membership in the Geological Society of London. As state geologist Rogers prepared a study called "Structure of the Appalachian Chain," which was recognized as one of the most important papers published by the Association of American Geological and Natural History. At the height of his powers he was said to be "without a peer among the scientific men of his age in addressing an intelligent and cultivated audience" and "his wave theory of the Mountain Chain was the first important contribution to dynamic and structural geology which had been brought forward in this country." Rogers's reputation was so great that Massachusetts invited him to come to Boston where he was largely responsible for the establishment of the Massachusetts Institute of Technology of which he served as president in his later years. He was an original

member of the National Academy of Sciences and served as
its president from 1878 to 1882.

Benjamin Henry Latrobe, son of a distinguished father,
was born in Philadelphia in 1806 and was graduated from
Georgetown College in Washington, D.C. He became one of
the leaders in the development and construction of early
railroads linking Baltimore and Washington with Ohio in
the Mississippi Valley. He made surveys of these lines and
designed and built the viaduct to Baltimore—Latrobe's Folly it was called—which "was recognized as one of the finest
pieces of railroad architecture in the country" and "was one
of the oldest railroad viaducts in the world successfully car-
rying modern equipment." In 1835 Latrobe became chief
engineer of the Baltimore and Post Deposit Railroad for
which he built a road from Baltimore to Havre de Grace.
That was followed by a survey and construction of a line
from Point of Rocks to Harpers Ferry in 1836, and thence
to Cumberland. In 1842 he was appointed chief engineer of
the Baltimore and Ohio, and in 1847 he extended the road
from Wheeling to Ohio. This in turn was followed by the
construction of 200 miles of track with 113 bridges and 11
tunnels that ultimately completed the Baltimore and Ohio
Railroad to Pittsburgh. Latrobe influenced the Magnetic
Telegraph Company to lay the first Morse line from Washington to Baltimore and Ohio. John Hazelton Latrobe,
brother of Benjamin, drafted the charter of the Baltimore
and Ohio Railroad, secured the right-of-way and recommended the installation of the first telegraph line from Baltimore to Washington. John Latrobe helped to found the
Maryland Institute for the Promotion of Mechanic Arts in
1825, promoted the Maryland Colonization Society, and
established the Liberia Colony in Africa. He was president
of the National Colonization Society for many years.

THREE

Journalists, Humorists, and the Theater

1. Journalists

FOR THE STUDENT OF THE OLD SOUTH, WHETHER HIS IN-
terest be politics, education, religion, economics, or general
knowledge, the newspapers of the period are of vital importance. More people read and depend on newspapers for
knowledge of their times than any other form of the printed
page. Realizing the hold the newspaper had upon the
average person, Thomas Jefferson said: "I would rather live
in a country with newspapers and without a government
than in a country with a government without newspapers."
Henry Ward Beecher described a newspaper as "a window
through which men look out on all that is going on in the
world. Without a newspaper a man is shut up in a small
room and knows little or nothing of what is happening outside of himself. In our day newspapers keep pace with history
and record it. A good newspaper will keep a sensible man in
sympathy with the world's current history." And Wendell
Phillips said, "Let me make the newspapers and I care not
who makes the religion or the laws."

Newspapers of the Old South, like those in the North, were
closely affiliated with one or the other of the two major
political parties; in fact patronage of a party was almost
necessary to ensure financial success of any paper. Since the
state legislatures chose the state printers, the political affiliation of an editor generally determined his election. It fol-

lowed that politics, debates in Congress and the state legislatures, and partisan political letters constituted a large part of the contents of the newspaper. Some editors, however, enlivened their columns with humorous stories, reports of police courts, essays, anecdotes, and even' poetry. The more liberal editors used their newspapers to advance democratic reforms in government, education in public schools and colleges, improvement of prison systems, and the establishment of institutions for the deaf, the dumb, and the blind.

A large number of Yankee editors, chiefly from New England and the Middle Atlantic states although there were a few from the Old Northwest, came to the South and established their own newspapers, or were employed by Southern newspaper owners. No one has compiled a list of Yankee editors in the South, but the number would certainly run into the hundreds, and they were found in every Southern state. They edited leading newspapers in Baltimore, Charleston, Mobile, New Orleans, Nashville, and Louisville and weekly papers in many small towns of the rural area. They made significant contributions to the life of their adopted states and region. Pen pictures of a representative group of Yankee editors will suffice to indicate their role in the life and society of the Old South.

Arunah Shepherdson Abell, born in Rhode Island in 1806, was affiliated with two Northern newspapers, the Providence *Patriot* in 1822 and the Philadelphia *Public Ledger* which he founded in 1836, before he moved to Maryland. He established the Baltimore *Sun* in 1837 and was sole proprietor and editor until 1868. The *Sun* was successful from the beginning and under Abell's editorship became one of the most influential newspapers in the nation. Abell was highly popular in Baltimore where he was an avid supporter of municipal reform and improvements. He was sympathetic with Southern mores, and the people trusted and supported him. In his efforts to serve the people's interest, Abell established the Pony Express to New Orleans in order that he might give immediate coverage of the Mexican War and of the Southwest in general. He was one of the first editors to use the telegraph to transmit news and the first to install the Hoe cylinder printing press. Abell employed Fulton Charles Carroll, a native of Pennsylvania who had served on the staff of the Philadelphia *National Gazette,* as manager of the *Sun.* After twelve years with the *Sun* Carroll purchased the Baltimore *American* in which he emphasized the development of the commercial interests of the South. When secession and Civil War came, Carroll supported the Union cause and his paper ceased to circulate in the Confederate states.

Hezekiah Niles was born in Pennsylvania in 1777 and moved to Baltimore, Maryland, in 1805 where he edited the *Apollo,* a literary journal, and the Baltimore *Evening Post.* He is best known, however, as the founder of *Niles' Weekly Register* of which he was editor for twenty-five years. In his earlier years Niles supported President Thomas Jefferson's views and policies, but in later life he became a strong champion of Henry Clay and Whig principles. Niles had opposed the recharter of the first Bank of the United States in 1811 but he supported the second Bank of the United States against President Andrew Jackson's drive to destroy it. He also came to favor protective tariffs and the gradual emancipation of slaves. *Niles' Weekly Register* was the leading journal of its type in the nation, and it continues to be a major source for the research scholar for the period of its existence. It has been described by one authority as "the most valuable newspaper of its day." Niles also edited *Principles and Acts of the Revolution in America,* an important source document for historians.

The Richmond *Enquirer,* under the editorship of Thomas Ritchie, and the Richmond *Whig,* under John Hampden Pleasants (Ritchie and Pleasants were native Virginians), had such a stranglehold on Virginia journalism that they overshadowed the smaller newspapers of the state. Despite such obstacles, however, Yankees established and edited newspapers which exerted considerable influence on the state. Anthony M. Keily, a native of New Jersey, founded the Norfolk *Virginian* and the Petersburg *Index and News*, both of which were important in eastern Virginia. Enos W. Newton, a Vermont Yankee, earnestly and successfully pleaded the cause of common school education in his Kanawha *Republican*. The Virginia-born editor of the *Valley Star* complained that the Yankee teachers in the area "exerted entirely too great an influence on education," but, in spite of his opposition, he admitted that they successfully continued their efforts for public schools. Ezra Bauder, a native of New York and a graduate of Union College, moved to Virginia and served as a tutor to John Marshall's grandsons, and later edited the Port Royal *Times* from 1854 to 1861. When the Civil War came, Bauder as a Northerner and Yankee "was viewed with suspicion and was arrested by a posse and taken to Fredericksburg." Some of his friends secured his release, but he was again arrested, tried, and acquitted. He then went to Richmond where he served as a Confederate government clerk. After the war he became a teacher in the Virginia public schools.

North Carolina, a backward rural state in the first half of the nineteenth century, nevertheless had some twenty-five newspapers in the 1830s, and the number had increased to more than fifty by 1860. Well over half the editors of these papers were Yankees, and among them were distinguished and influential journalists. Among the more important was Joseph Gales, a native of England where he had attained distinction as an editor and champion of individual rights and freedom. Forced to leave England, Gales migrated to Pennsylvania where he added to his fame as an editor. Moving to North Carolina, Gales established the Raleigh *Register*, which soon became one of the most important papers in the state. Among other Yankee editors of note in North Carolina were Dennis Heart, a native of Connecticut, who established and edited the Hillsborough *Recorder;* Thomas Loring of Massachusetts, who edited the Wilmington *Herald;* William

Boylan of New Jersey, who established and edited the *North Carolina Minerva* and the Fayetteville *Gazette;* and Philo White of New York, who was editor of the Raleigh *Standard.* The editor of the Raleigh *Times* made a study of the relation of Yankee editors in the state to slavery. He found that all of those who became slaveholders were strong supporters of the institution, while those who owned no slaves were either lukewarm in support or outspoken in oppostion to the institution. He found also that the wealthy slaveholding planters rather than the nonslaveholding yeomen farmers were the chief subscribers to the newspapers. Boylan, in addition to his interest in journalism, was president of the state bank, a trustee of the Raleigh Academy, a member of the commission which supervised the building of the state capitol in 1831, an advocate of internal improvements, and a leader in the building of the North Carolina Railroad in 1848.

The Charleston *Courier* was one of the most important newspapers in antebellum South Carolina. It was founded by Loring Andrews of Hingham, Massachusetts, who, before moving to South Carolina, had gained a wide reputation as editor of the *Western Star* in Stockbridge and the *Herald of Freedom* in Boston. Andrews edited the *Courier* from 1800 to 1807 and developed it into "one of the most influential commercial newspapers" in the South. Aaron S. Willington was the proprietor and publisher of the *Courier.* He brought James Gordon Bennett to the staff in 1823. Willington began to board vessels from Havana, Cuba, and get newspapers which had been brought from Spain which arrived earlier than those from London, Le Havre, and Liverpool, and was thus able to scoop the newspapers which relied on the English line. The Charleston *Courier* took a strong stand against the rising tide of sectionalism in South Carolina in the 1820s and 1830s. One contemporary writer described the *Courier* as "bristling with denuniciation of anything and everything that could be interpreted as tending toward disunion." It thus challenged the Charleston *Mercury* on this issue. The *Courier* continued to emphasize the importance of union versus nullification and secession throughout the controversy over states' rights and sectionalism.

A similar conflict developed between the newspapers of Georgia where a large percentage of the editors and their papers were closely allied with the nullifiers of South Carolina. In fact a goodly number of the Georgia editors had been born in South Carolina. The lineup was also one of Democrats versus Whigs in Georgia. Among the Yankee Whig editors in Georgia who opposed the South Carolina extremists in the 1840s and 1850s were Daniel Lee who edited the Augusta *Chronicle*, J. L. Locke of the Savannah *Republican* (which, incidentally, had the largest circulation of any newspaper in the state in 1850), and Dr. L. F. W. Andrews, editor of the Macon *Citizen*. Leading Democratic papers, including the Milledgeville *Federal Union* and the Augusta *Constitutionalist*, insisted that Lee be forced to resign from his editorship because of his Yankee antislavery and anti–states' rights philosophy. But the publisher supported Lee in a formal statement, and he and the moderate faction won the fight for the Union cause in Georgia in 1850. In 1860 Lee served as one of the secretaries of the Constitutional Union Party Convention and also as a member of the executive committee.

Despite the French influence in Louisiana some of the better newspapers of New Orleans during the first half of the nineteenth century were owned and edited by Yankees. J. W. Frost, who had made a reputation as an orator in Maine, moved to New Orleans where he became editor of the *Crescent*. The editor of the *Commercial Bulletin* was a Connecticut Yankee and a graduate of Yale College.

George Wilkins Kendall, a New England Yankee, had two entirely different careers, the first as a journalist in New Orleans and the second as the owner and manager of a sheep ranch in Texas; he was highly successful in both. Kendall was born in Mount Vernon, New Hampshire, in 1809 and began his journalistic career with the Amherst *Herald*. He held that position for a short time, and then moved rapidly to the Boston *Statesman,* the Washington *United States Telegraph,* the *National Intelligencer,* and the Mobile *Register.* In January 1837 he settled in New Orleans where he founded and edited the *Picayune* and gained a national reputation as a humorist. In 1841 Mirabeau Bonaparte Lamar, president of the Republic of Texas, planned an expedition to Santa Fe to open trade and to encourage northern Mexico to join Texas. Kendall accompanied this expedition as a reporter. He was captured and held prisoner in Mexico for several months. While in prison Kendall wrote letters to the *Picayune* which aroused interest throughout the United States. His *Narrative of the Texan Santa Fe Expedition* became immensely popular and sold some forty thousand copies in eight years. On this expedition Kendall became an enthusiastic supporter of the admission of Texas to the Union. He was with Gen. Winfield Scott's army on the march from Vera Cruz to Mexico City in the war with Mexico, and his reporting of that campaign entitles him to rank as the first modern war correspondent. In order that his reports might reach the *Picayune* in time for it to give the first news of the campaign and its battles, Kendall hired express couriers to carry his dispatches to New Orleans. Kendall's *War between the United States and Mexico* was a popular work and had good sales.

In 1845, Kendall bought a sheep ranch of some forty thousand acres. He stocked the ranch with ewes from Mexico and France and Merino rams from Vermont. In 1853 he added Leicester sheep and hired Joseph Tait, a Scot, as his manager. The *Texas Almanac* of 1853 said that if Kendall could "go for another year, with the same extraordinary success [experienced] in the two just passed, he will have incontestably proven the fact that no better sheep ranch exists in the wide world than his," and that he "would become the greatest sheep man Texas ever claimed."

Kendall, as did most Yankees who made their homes in the South, became an ardent champion of slavery. He defended the doctrine of states' rights and could find little, if anything, good to say about abolitionists. He wrote to his friend Henry S. Randall of New York that James Buchanan was the weakest of presidents. Buchanan, said Kendall, "looked timidly on while half a dozen Northern States, your own among the number, have virtually nullified—have openly trampled the Constitution under foot by their action in regard to the Fugitive Slave Law." He noted also that Northerners preached the higher law and the irrepressible conflict doctrines. Kendall was not a secessionist but said that the entire South should "hold council together, decide upon a firm and dignified plan of action, give the North an unmistakable ultimatum and in the meantime prepare for the worst. . . . If you in the North openly nullify by setting aside a plain and palpable provision of the Constitution, any State in the South has an undoubted right to secede." When war came in 1861, Kendall declared that the "deceit and double dealing of Abraham Lincoln [were] duplicity and double dealing which would have disgraced the Mexican Santa Anna, be a match for Satan himself, and shame even a Comanche [Indian]." Kendall did not participate actively in the Civil War, but he offered the wool from his ranch to the Confederate quartermaster general and shipped wool to a Confederate post in New Orleans until that city fell to the federal forces. In writing Kendalls's obituary, Henry Randall said that Kendall "loved Texas with absolute devotion. He never was tired of writing or speaking its praise."

Samuel Bangs was born in Boston in 1794, but little is known of his early years. In 1816 he appeared in Baltimore as a printer. From there he sailed to Mexico where he joined a group of Mexican revolutionaries whose aim was Mexican independence. Bangs was captured, held prisoner at Saltillo, and was forced to work at a government press. After his release in 1828 Bangs became a printer for the Texas provinces. In 1835 he joined Benjamin Lundy in a plan to establish a colony of free Negroes in Texas. Bangs secured a grant of land from the Republic of Texas and Lundy returned to the United States hoping to raise funds for the project. He was unsuccessful and the colony failed to materialize.

After the organization of the Texas republic, Bangs devoted his full time to journalism and was the founder and publisher of a series of short-lived newspapers. Among them were the *Galvestonian,* the San Luis *Advocate,* the Galveston *Texas Times,* the *Commercial Intelligencer,* the *Independent Chronicle,* and the *Daily Globe.* In these journals Bangs was often at odds with President Sam Houston and hardly qualified as a loyal opponent. Bangs's "persistent demands for adequate defense against Mexico won for him many friends," but, said the *Commercial Intelligencer,* "the Yankee Printer's voice was not the only one raised against the Houston administration." Bangs also attacked Houston for having "declared E. W. Moore the Commander of the Texas Navy an outlaw" and, to show his resentment, Bangs gave Moore a public dinner.

On October 15, 1843, Bangs announced in the *Chronicle* that the "leading features of our political department will be a *firm* and *decided* stand against the *prominent measures* and *policy* of the present administration; believing that with a fair and *impartial* presentation of *facts,* without personal or rancorous abuse of party, that we will be able to convince the honest and intelligent People, that such measures and such policy are not only in opposition to the best interest of our country, but subversive of the fundamental principles on which our government is founded."

Bangs continued his attacks upon the administration and carried the fight to the military. On New Year's Day, 1846, he established the Corpus Christi *Gazette,* called by some writers "the first war newspaper." Moving the press to Matamoros on June 24, 1846, Bangs published the *Reveille,* with the slogan, "The People of this Continent alone have the right to decide their destiny." The paper was printed in a pro-Mexican shop and Gen. Zachary Taylor ordered the shop closed and the editor arrested. Bangs protested, correct-

ly, that the slogan was taken from the Monroe Doctrine and
that he had committed no offense. Even so his paper was
killed, and Bangs removed to Kentucky where he died in
1854. Bangs had established the first press in Texas and the
official organ in three of the Mexican states. A man of enterprising spirit, courage, and ability, he took pride in his work
and contributed much to the development and progress of
the press in Mexico and Texas.

In the mid-1830s Democratic party leaders in Tennessee
sought an aggressive editor for their chief newspaper, the
Nashville *Union.* James K. Polk was chosen to find such a
journalist, and he selected Jeremiah George Harris, a native
of Connecticut, who had been editor of the Massachusetts
Bay State Democrat. Harris became editor of the *Union* in 1839
and conducted an aggressive attack upon the Whig opposition. It was said of him that "in ability to distort the truth
and to engage in vituperative castigation of his political
opponents he was exceeded in the antebellum period [in
Tennessee] only by the Whig editor . . . Parson William G.
Brownlow." Harris charged that John Bell, a Whig leader,
had joined the abolitionists in voting in Congress for resolutions to prevent the discussion of slavery. Whereupon A. A.
Hall, editor of the Nashville *Banner,* a Whig mouthpiece,
charged that Harris had been an abolitionist while editor of
the New Bedford *Daily Gazette* and had bitterly condemned
Southern slaveholders in his editorials. In his countercharge
Harris obscured the issue and extricated himself from a difficult situation. Later Harris directed a bitter attack upon Sen.
Ephraim H. Foster, whereupon Foster's son attacked Harris
and shot him in his arm, breast, and jaw, and so disabled him
that Harris retired from the editorship of the *Union.* John P.
Heiss, a Pennsylvanian and an editor of some repute and
standing, succeeded Harris as editor of the *Union.* In 1839 the
Argus, a Democratic paper, was established in Knoxville, and
Elbridge Eastman, a native of New Hampshire, was chosen
its editor.

Yankee editors also found their way to and made their mark in Missouri. Franklin Nathaniel Patton, a native of Massachusetts, moved to Franklin, Missouri. He ordered a press from New York City which he hauled by wagon over miserably bad roads the two hundred miles from St. Louis to Franklin. Patton published the first number of the *Missouri Intelligencer and Boon's Lick Advertiser* in 1819, the first American newspaper published west of St. Louis. The *Intelligencer* ceased publication in 1835. A man of energy, candor, and intelligence, Patton published a weekly paper of exemplary quality. E. W. Stephen, president of the Missouri Press Association, said that Patton "deserved to be canonized as the pioneer, the path finder, the Moses of country journalism in Missouri."

George Dennison Prentice was born in Connecticut in 1802, was graduated from Brown University, studied law and was admitted to the bar, but chose journalism as a career. He edited the New London *Mirror* from 1825 to 1828 and then became the first editor of the Hartford *New England Review* in 1828. He moved to Louisville, Kentucky, in 1830 where he became editor of the *Daily Journal,* a position he held until 1868. Under his leadership the *Journal* became one of the most influential Whig newspapers of the South and West. Honest, intelligent and fearless, Prentice was recognized as one of the ablest editors of the mid-nineteenth century. He was one of those Yankees who, "originally educated to think slavery morally wrong," changed his opinion when he became familiar with the institution at firsthand and publicly recanted. He editorialized: "We think that where the climate and soil are favorable the blacks are better off in slavery than out of it. We wish to see it left everywhere to the will of the whites and the operation of natural causes."

A Whig in politics, Prentice was an ardent supporter of Henry Clay for the presidency. He published a campaign biography of Henry Clay in 1831. Prentice collected and published in 1860 a volume of his editorials under the title

Prenticieana, a sort of Bible for the old-line Whigs. His editorials and short squibs were noted for their keen wit, satire, and abuse.

Prentice was a loyal Unionist in 1860 and, although his son enlisted and fought in the Confederate Army, was influential in keeping Kentucky loyal to the Union. In the fierce conflict between Confederate and Union feeling an ardent Confederate supporter pulled down the United States flag flying over the *Journal* building. Prentice ordered one of the staff to "go up on the roof and throw the scoundrel down among the mob." A student at the University of Virginia, a Mr. Lake who was a subscriber to the *Journal,* wrote Prentice on May 17, 1861: "Stop my paper; I can't afford to read abbolition [sic] journals in these times; the atmosphere of Old Virginia will not admit of such filthy sheets as yours has grown to be." To which Prentice replied: "Lake, I think it a great pity that a young man should go to a university to graduate a traitor and a blackguard—and so ignorant as to spell abolition with two b's." Even in such tempestuous times Prentice made effective use of his sharp wit and stinging satire. Prentice did not himself follow the Republican party and Abraham Lincoln on abolition, but he supported wholeheartedly the Lincoln administration on major issues and was overjoyed when the Union was saved.

2. Humorists and Sentimental Novelists

During the 1830s a group of Yankee writers emerged in the Southern states who wrote humorously and realistically about life as they saw it. They knew frontier settlers, the poor whites, the middle-class yeoman farmers, the new rich whom Daniel R. Hundley called "Cotton Slobs," and the wealthy planter class. From their writings one can get a good cross section of the Southern social order and of the intermingling of the classes. Their tall tales, grotesque exaggerations, and descriptions of happenings in the daily life of the people make delightful reading. These writers did not hesitate to poke fun at social customs, the economic order, religious concepts, and political patterns. Much of this type of writing needs to be read aloud to be fully appreciated, for the authors used phonetic spelling and the crude dialect of the Southern backwoods farmer and poor white. The dean of this school of writers was Augustus Baldwin Longstreet, a native Georgian, a Yale graduate, a lawyer and a journalist who turned Methodist minister. Thinking his *Georgia Scenes* beneath the dignity of one of God's chosen spokesman, Longstreet attempted to buy and burn all copies of his book. Fortunately, he failed. His alma mater honored him with an honorary degree, and his name comes down to us with his delightful stories of the Georgia people.

The Yankee writers found an outlet for their racy tales in William T. Porter's *Spirit of the Times* published in New York. Representative of the many such writers were Thomas Bangs Thorpe, William Tappan Thompson, and George W. Harris. Thorpe was born in Massachusetts in 1815, was graduated from Wesleyan University, and removed to Louisiana in 1835. From 1843 to 1850 he edited the *New Orleans Commercial Times and Daily Topic.* He served as a colonel in the Mexican War and became a close friend of Zachary Taylor. Thorpe was an artist and painted portraits of President Taylor and Jenny Lind. But Thorpe's most significant works are his sketches and books, ten in number, on Southern frontier life. He is described as having "a genuine relish for the sports and pastimes of Southern frontier life, and described them with remarkable freshness and skill. . . . No one enters into all the whims and grotesque humours of the backwoodsman or brings him more accurately or clearly before us." "The Big Bear of Arkansas," which was published in 1841 in the *Spirit of the Times,* and also in book form, is one of Thorpe's most humorous, racy, and significant stories. *Tom Owen, the Bee-Hunter,* published in 1854, won international acclaim in England and was translated into French, Italian, and German. Other popular books by

Thorpe were *The Master's House: A Tale of Southern Life,* which
was published in 1854, and *The Mysteries of the Backwoods; or,
Sketches of the Southwest: Including Character, Scenery, and Rural
Sports,* published in 1846. Thorpe loved the South but was
loyal to the Union and in 1861 served as a colonel of vol-
unteers under Gen. Benjamin F. Butler.

William Tappan Thompson was born in Ohio in 1812 and
moved to Florida where he served as an assistant to James
D. Wescott, secretary of the Florida Territory. Moving to
Augusta, Georgia, in 1835 he accepted a post on the Augusta
State Rights Sentinel. Under the tutelage of Augustus Baldwin
Longstreet, Thompson began to write sketches similar to
those which Longstreet had made famous. Over the years he
published seven volumes of such sketches. In 1843 he published *Major Jones Courtship,* which was republished in Philadelphia under the title *Major Jones's Chronicles of Pineville* in
1843. In 1848 Thompson published a third volume titled
Major Jones Sketches and Travel. These stories give an excellent
picture of rural social life in Georgia. Jones, the uneducated,
unsophisticated rustic, chewed tobacco and expectorated everywhere. But he courted a Wesleyan college student and
introduced her to the sport of possum hunting. *Major Jones
Courtship* was exceedingly popular and sold more than fifteen
thousand copies in the first year. Thompson became a supporter of slavery and published *The Slaveholder Abroad,* a sympathetic picture of plantation aristocracy.

George Washington Harris was born in Pennsylvania in
1814 and moved to Tennessee in 1823. With little or no
formal schooling Harris had an interesting, varied, and remarkable career. He was at various times a mechanic, steamboat captain, postmaster of Knoxville, coal miner, railroad
engineer, journalist, and writer. He is best known, however,
as the author of *Sut Lovingood Yarns,* published in 1867. His
characters are tremendous, and "Sut's Daddy Playing
Horse," "The Biled Shirt," and "Parson Bullen's Lizzards"
are sidesplitting stories. Those who have never read Harris's

yarns are missing a delightful experience. Harris first published his yarns in local newspapers, but in 1843 William T.
Porter, editor of the New York *Spirit of the Times,* suggested
that Harris write for Porter's paper, but that he adopt "Sug-
artail" as a pseudonym. However, Harris preferred "Sut
Lovingood," and his yarns were carried under his preferred
pseudonym in the *Spirit of the Times* from 1843 to 1857. Indigenous to the South, the work of the sketch writers consti-
tutes a significant contribution to American literature. In
1852 the editor of the London *Westminster Review* wrote, "For
vivid imagination, comic plot, Rabelaisian touch, and sheer
fun, *The Sut Lovingood Yarns* surpass anything in American
humor: We know not where to turn for anything more rich,
original, indigenous, than much of the racy mockery and
grotesque extravagance of their pages."

The 1850s, the "feminine fifties" as they were called, saw
the rise and popularity of the sentimental novel, dripping in
saccharine sweetness. They told of love and marriage, of
desertion and divorce, and of retribution and reward. Of
little literary merit the novels were so similar in plot and
story that many writers turned them out by the scores. Wom-
en were the chief authors but men were also guilty of palm-
ing off this trash on the public. And why not? They sold
extremely well, and the profits were phenomenal. It was
reported that one writer wrote twenty such books in one year
and eighty in a ten-year period. These writings were of little
lasting merit but they represent a stage in American literature. They are important also because of the considerable
influence they exerted on that literary period. The writers of
the novels were not limited to one area but were found in the
North, South, East, and West.

Carolyn Lee Hentz, a native of Massachusetts, moved
with her husband to North Carolina, where he was a professor of French in the state university. Carolyn evidently had
some literary talent, for she won a prize of five hundred
dollars for one of her plays which was produced in the lead-

ing theaters, North and South. Seeing a more golden opportunity she turned to writing love stories—"Courtship and Marriage," "Lovell's Folly," and "The Planter's Northern Bride"—sixteen in all. In *The Planter's Northern Bride* she presented slavery as a beneficent social arrangement on the ground that it gave the planter's bride the advantage of well-trained and loyal household servants.

Mary Jane Holmes, a native of Massachusetts who had moved to Kentucky, wrote more than thirty sentimental love stories of which she claimed to have sold more than two million copies. Her *Tempest and Sunshine,* a story of personality clashes between two sisters, was on the best seller list for four years. *Lena Rivers,* another of Mrs. Holmes's books, also made the preferred list. But Joseph Holt Ingraham, born in Maine in 1809 and a graduate of Bowdoin College, beat Mrs. Hentz and Mrs. Holmes at their own game. He moved to Louisiana where he was a tutor in a planter family. The next year he moved to Mississippi and became a professor at Jefferson College. He published his first book, *The Southwest by a Yankee,* in two volumes, in 1835. It was a first-rate contemporary account of the region. He next wrote a fictionalized biography of *LaFitte the Pirate.* He also wrote two other books dealing with the Old South—*The Sunny South,* an account of a tutoress, and *The Quadroone.* Ingraham then turned to the love story and in ten years, 1835 to 1845, he published eighty works. Henry Wadsworth Longfellow, who knew Ingraham personally, wrote facetiously: "He [Ingraham] is tremendous—really tremendous. I think one may say that he writes the worst novels ever written by anybody. But they sell; he says he gets twelve hundred dollars apiece." At the temporary rate for such books Ingraham had royalties of a least three thousand dollars per year. Ingraham was also one of the early novelists to write on the religious theme. His *Prince of the House of David* dealt with the birth of Christ, *The Pillow of Fire* with Israel in bondage, and *The Throne of David* with the land of Canaan and Absalom's rebellion.

Carolyn Howard Gilman, a native of Boston who moved to Charleston, South Carolina, with her husband Samuel Gilman, a Unitarian minister, wrote widely on Southern life. She edited two literary periodicals, the *Southern Rose* for women and the *Rosebud* for girls. Mrs. Gilman's *Recollections of a Housekeeper* recounts the prosaic happenings of her early life, and her *Recollection of a New England Bride and a Southern Matron* is a pale forerunner of Mrs. Franklin D. Roosevelt's *My Day*. Mrs. Gilman's *Poetry of Traveling in the United States* is gracefully written and gives a humorous account of life in the North and the South. Her volume *Oracles from the Poets* was well received and went through several editions.

Two Southern Yankees, Margaret Junkin Preston and Albert Pike, were prolific writers and highly popular in their day. Margaret Junkin was the daughter of George Junkin, a Pennsylvanian who became president of Washington College, now Washington and Lee University. Margaret married Prof. John T. L. Preston, the founder of the Virginia Military Institute. She contributed numerous stories and poems to magazines and won several prizes. But she was unhappy in the community because she was not immediately accepted. After her marriage she became a strong Southern sympathizer. Her first book *Silverwood* was published anonymously, although her publisher offered her two hundred dollars if she would let him use her name. Her second book *Beechwood* was very popular and sold eight thousand copies within one year.

Albert Pike was born in Massachusetts in 1809. He studied at Harvard College, which bestowed upon him an honorary master of arts degree, and then he moved to Arkansas at the age of twenty-four. Pike was a man of many parts. He taught school, engaged in trade with the Indians, studied law, and was admitted to practice law in the United States Supreme Court. At different times Pike edited the Arkansas *Advocate* and the Memphis *Appeal*. He also served as the commander of a cavalry troop in the Mexican War and as brigadier

general in the Confederate States Army during the Civil
War. A historian of Arkansas described Pike in the following
manner: "Foremost among lawyers of the period for his
intellectual attainments no less than for his political and
military exploits, must be the commanding figure of Albert
Pike." In addition to the achievements named above, Pike
had considerable stature as a writer. His *Narrative of a Journey
in the Prairie* is an interesting account of frontier life. His *Prose
Sketches and Poems Written in the Western Country* are reminiscent
of and dominated by the community in which his life was
cast. But Pike's reputation as a poet rests largely on his *Hymns
to the Gods* which won high praise at home and abroad. Christopher North, editor of Blackwood's *Edinburgh Magazine,*
wrote: "These fine hymns entitle the author to take his place
in the highest order of his country's poets." Pike, like most
writers, served his day and generation well, but his name is
now hardly known except in his own state.

3.   The Southern Theater
The first recorded theatrical performance in the English
colonies in America took place in Accomac County, Virginia, in 1665 when three local citizens presented *Ye Bare and Ye
Cub.* The next known production, a pastoral colloquy, was
recited by the students of the College of William and Mary
at Williamsburg, Virginia, in 1702. A third performance was
given in Charleston, South Carolina, by Anthony Ashton, a
British playwright in 1703. Ashton described this act as follows: "Well we arrived in Charlestown, full of Lice, Shame,
Poverty, Nakedness and Hunger:—I turned *Player* and Poet,
and wrote one Play on the Subject of the Country." In such
minor performances the theater in the United States had its
beginnings.
     During the colonial period puritan thought and influence
were unfavorable to the development of the theater in New
England, but, sanctioned by the Anglican church, the theater enjoyed popularity in the Southern colonies. After the

American Revolution the theater grew more rapidly in the large Northern cities than in the rural South. Consequently, many of the leaders in the development of the theater in the Old South were Yankees who had won recognition on the Northern circuit as actors or theater managers. Noah Miller Ludlow and Solomon Franklin Smith, both natives of New York, were two of the most influential men in the development of the Southern theater in the first half of the nineteenth century, and their careers were remarkably similar. After having established themselves in their profession, Ludlow and Smith joined forces in 1835, and from then until 1853, when they dissolved partnership, they dominated the theater in the South and West. Their chief competitor was James H. Caldwell, an English actor and manager, who built an American theater in New Orleans in 1822 which was highly successful and, for a time, rivaled the French opera in popularity in New Orleans. Both Ludlow and Smith wrote accounts of their careers which constitute the best contemporary sources on the theater in the Old South.

Ludlow was born in New York City in 1795 and died in St. Louis in 1886. He began his career as a member of Samuel Drake's Theatrical Company in 1815 and played the circuit through Pennsylvania, Kentucky, and Tennessee. In 1817 Ludlow organized his own company and played the small towns up and down the Mississippi River from New Orleans to St. Louis. In 1818 he gave what is generally regarded as the first theatrical performance in English in the New Orleans theater. Ludlow thus aroused a desire for an English theater and laid the foundation for a remarkable development of the theater in the Crescent City. In 1823 he played under gaslights in the New American Theatre, the first theater so lighted west of the Appalachian Mountains and two years ahead of the New York theaters. He then extended his circuit through Mississippi to Mobile, Alabama, where George Handell Hill played his exceedingly popular role in *The Yankee. Ludlow's Dramatic Life As I Found*

It: A Record of Personal Experience, published in 1880, despite
its inaccuracies and the author's effort to prove that he was
the first to introduce the professional theater in the towns of
the Southwest, has been characterized by one critic as "well-
nigh invaluable in the history of the American stage" and by
another as "the most important account of the western theatre by a competent observer."

Sol Smith was born in Norwich, New York, in 1808 and
died in St. Louis in 1869. As a young man he moved to
Cincinnati, where he founded and edited, for a short time,
the *Independent Press and Freedom's Advocate.* But his real interest
was the theater, and he soon abandoned the press and began
his theatrical career as a strolling player and manager. Like
Ludlow, Smith joined Caldwell's troupe and played the circuit up and down the Mississippi River. After his first season
he organized a small troupe of his own and played many of
the towns of Mississippi, Tennessee, Alabama, and Georgia.
In the small rural towns he encountered the bitter opposition
of the Methodist and Baptist clergy. Smith wrote that the
"evangelists endeavoured to make their hearers believe that
all who attended the theatre would certainly be roasted in
the hottest sort of fires." Consequently, Smith's early performances were lacking in financial success. At Tuscaloosa,
Alabama, Smith decided to fight fire with fire and gave a
scene from *Don Juan: The Libertine Destroyed,* which showed
fiends in red and blue flames in which the wicked suffered
death. But this effort reacted against him, for the flames set
the small theater building on fire, and it burned to the
ground. The ministers used this incident as a sure sign that
God was on their side, and they intensified their attacks. But
the tide soon turned. The audiences increased in numbers,
and Smith recorded in his diary that the ministers continued
to criticize and abuse him. But, he said, "We got the Money."

Smith organized his Independent Theatre Troupe of the
Southwestern States in 1831. He, as did Ludlow, had some
success with their strolling companies, but they soon found

that with their limited resources they could not compete successfully with Caldwell, whose company was well established and financed. Hence in 1835 they joined forces as Ludlow and Smith with St. Louis and Mobile as their respective bases and found that they could compete with Caldwell. When Caldwell opened his new American Theatre, "elegant in design and architecture," in 1842, Ludlow and Smith countered with their New St. Charles Theatre in New Orleans in 1843. Shortly thereafter the American Theatre burned, and Ludlow and Smith found themselves dominant over theatrical affairs in St. Louis, New Orleans, and Mobile. The New York *Spirit of the Times,* of July 8, 1843, declared that Ludlow and Smith "have under their direction three of the largest and most beautiful theaters in the country, and feel disposed to offer the most liberal terms to talented members of the profession." Thereafter, Ludlow and Smith brought the leading stars to their theaters, among whom were Edwin and Junius Booth, Charlotte Cushman, Fanny Essler, Anna Cora Ogden, Jenny Lind, Edwin Forest, Tyrone Power, Joseph Jefferson, Charles and Ellen Kean, and Charles Macready. Another reporter wrote that Ludlow and Smith had "several clever people in their company besides *all the Stars in Creation.*" They "not only dominate the theater history of the South [he said] but also build reputations second to none in the United States." The Columbus, Georgia, *Enquirer* declared: "We doubt whether any other company in the United States, enlivened our inland villages and combine as much talent for tragic and comic acting . . . as does Old Sol's." And the St. Louis press characterized Ludlow and Smith as "men of respectability, as attentive managers and citizens, . . . gentlemen who have real claims upon this community."

Smith's *Theatrical Management in the West and South for Thirty Years,* which was published in 1868, is an interesting and important source on the development of the theater in the Old South. One should read it, however, with a critical attitude, for Smith often exaggerated and overemphasized his contributions to the theater.

Anna Cora Ogden Ritchie, a New York Yankee, deserves recognition for her contributions to the Old South on two counts: first on her role as an actress and writer and second on her work in establishing the Mount Vernon Association, which was largely responsible in preserving George Washington's home, Mount Vernon, as a national shrine. Born in Bordeaux, France, in 1819, where her father, a native of New York, was stationed in government service, she was twice married, first to James Mowatt and second to William Foushee Ritchie of Richmond, Virginia, in 1854.

Mrs. Ritchie wrote numerous articles for *Godeys Lady's Book, Graham's Magazine,* and other similar periodicals. Her fiction, like that of most of the novels of the "feminine fifties," was dripping with saccharine sentimentality, but if it had little or no lasting literary value, it filled the wants of the day and generation. Her *Clergyman's Wife and Other Sketches* is a good example. Her *Autobiography of an Actress; or, Eight Years on the Stage* was read in manuscript by her husband Ritchie, edited by Epes Sargent, and published by Tichnor and Fields of Boston in 1854.

Anna Mowatt made her stage debut in Boston's Park Theatre as Pauline in *The Lady of Lyons* in 1845. She played *The Stranger* on her major theatrical tour of 1853 which carried her from the Boston theater to New York, Richmond, Charleston, Mobile, New Orleans, and Memphis. Her most popular individual appearance was in *Juliet* in Boston in 1854, when seats were auctioned at twenty dollars each.

When Ann Pamela Cunningham of Richmond, Virginia, in 1855 determined to rescue, restore, and preserve Mount Vernon as a national shrine, she invited Mrs. Ritchie to join in the undertaking. As secretary to the central committee, Mrs. Ritchie threw herself into the work with enthusiasm and determination. She gave a party to which she invited Gov. John B. Floyd and a large number of members of both

houses of the Virginia legislature. After an "excellent program of music," Mrs. Ritchie served "good wine and turtle
soup" and, needless to say, secured sufficient signatures from
the legislators to insure introduction and passage of the bill
and the establishment of the Mount Vernon Association.
Mrs. Ritchie's biographer says of this lobbying that "for the
first time in [Virginia's] history it became legal for women
to band together for legal action." Be that as it may, Mrs.
Ritchie had been largely responsible for the legislation. She
then prevailed on her friend Edward Everett, the great Boston orator, to speak in support of the association. On this
occasion some seventy thousand dollars were raised, and the
work of restoration was begun. For her role in this undertaking Mrs. Ritchie was made vice-regent of the Mount Vernon
Ladies Association.

FOUR

Religious Leaders

A GLANCE AT THE RELIGIOUS ESTABLISHMENT AT THE BE-
ginning of the American Revolution will show that the Congregational church was the leading one in New England,
with the Baptists dominant in Rhode Island; the Presbyterian church was strongest in the Middle Atlantic region, with
Quakers in control in Pennsylvania; and the Episcopal
church was the established one in the South, except in Maryland where religious toleration prevailed. Methodists, Baptists, and a number of other sects were found in small
numbers throughout the South. Their membership was
made up primarily of the lower economic class and was
generally looked down upon by the members of the more
favored Episcopal church. During the Revolutionary War,
however, it was difficult to prevent the bolder members of the
dissenting sects from ignoring the authority of the established
church. For instance, Daniel Marshall, a Vermont Yankee
and a Baptist preacher in Georgia, was arrested in 1771,
tried, convicted, and ordered not to preach in the state. He
replied to the order, "Whether it be right to obey God or
man, judge ye." But as for himself, he would obey God's will,
not that of the Episcopal church nor the government. He
continued his ministry and established the first Baptist
church in Georgia, and in 1784 presided over the organization of a Georgia Baptist association.

Yankee dissenters in South Carolina chose to work
through more orderly channels. William Tennent, a Presbyterian, and Richard Furman, a Baptist, were leaders in

91

the fight for disestablishment by constitutional revision. Tennent was born in Ireland in 1705 and settled in New Jersey where he became a Presbyterian minister in 1732. He moved to South Carolina before the Revolution and became minister of the Independent Church in Charleston. He was selected by a public meeting of dissenters to present a petition to the state legislature, of which he was a member, which asked for "freedom from religious tyranny and ecclesiastical oppressions." Aided by Oliver Hart, a Yankee from Pennsylvania, and Richard Furman from New York, both Baptists, Tennent drew up a petition calling on the legislature to grant equality to all protestants. The petition reads in part as follows: "That there shall never be the establishment of any one Denomination or sect of Protestants by way of preference to another in this state . . . but that all Protestants shall enjoy free and equal privileges, both religious and civil." Christopher Gadsden presented the petition, and Tennent discussed and defended it in the legislature. The petition was adopted in 1778, and all protestants were guaranteed equal rights. Similar action took place in other Southern states.

The civil-ecclesiastical connection had existed in the South prior to the Revolution, but when it was abolished voluntarily, financial support became necessary for the Episcopal church. That church had suffered a loss of leadership since many of the Anglican clergy left the South after the Revolution, and it became difficult for the church to find a sufficient number of priests to supply its parishes. As late as 1835 Moses Ashley Curtis, a native of Massachusetts and a graduate of Williams College, moved to North Carolina as a missionary of the Episcopal church. Furthermore, the establishment of the Methodist Episcopal Society, later to be the Methodist Episcopal church, as a separate organization weakened the Protestant Episcopal church in the South. In fact religious interest generally declined during and immediately after the Revolution. The destruction of church property and the loss of ministers contributed to this end, and the

Samuelson
Kurt

Poly a Econ Add

pressure of economic and political reorganization tended to push religious interest into the background. In North Carolina, for example, the Reverend Eli Caruthers, a Presbyterian minister, said in 1800 that "men of education and especially the young men of the country think it is a mark of independence to scoff at the Bible and the professors of religion." Joseph Caldwell, who removed from New Jersey to North Carolina to become a professor at the University of North Carolina, said: "In North Carolina, particularly in that part that lies east of the University, everyone believes that the first step he ought to take to rise in respectability is to disown, as often and publicly as he can, all regard for the leading doctrines of the Scriptures." He hastened to add, however, that in New Jersey "the Church had the public respect and support."

Weakened by disestablishment and loss of clergy, the Episcopal church made serious efforts to regain its former position of leadership in the South. The Reverend Charles Pettigrew, a native of Pennsylvania who had become the rector of St. Paul's Parish in Edenton, North Carolina, reorganized the Protestant Episcopal church in North Carolina in the 1790s. He called a general convention of the church in 1792 and was elected the first bishop of the Episcopal church in the state in 1795, but was never consecrated in the office.

Other Yankee bishops who contributed to the rebuilding and strengthening of the Episcopal church in the South were Richard Channing Moore and Charles Todd Quintard. Moore, a native of New York, studied medicine at King's College and theology under Bishop Samuel Provost. He became a popular minister and was rector at some of the leading churches in New York City. He moved to Monumental Church in Richmond, Virginia, in 1814, and was consecrated bishop of Virginia in the same year. Moore rendered notable service in reviving the fortunes of the Episcopal church in Virginia. He was active in restoring discipline in the church, and established new churches and increased the

number of clergy. He also established an Episcopal school
and the Virginia Episcopal Seminary, and he published *The
Doctrines of the Church.* The church under his leadership had
a "record of continual advancement and triumph in Virginia." Quintard, born in Connecticut, was trained in medicine
at the New York Medical College and became professor at
the Memphis Medical College in 1849. He also edited the
Memphis *Medical Record.* Abandoning the medical profession, Quintard was ordained a priest in the Protestant Episcopal church and became rector at the Memphis Calvary
Church in 1856. Like most Yankees in the South, he cast his
lot with the Confederacy and served in the Confederate
Army as chaplain. He was elected a bishop of the Episcopal
church in 1865. Quintard reopened the University of the
South, which had been closed during the Civil War, and
served as its chancellor from 1868 to 1872.

Daniel Stephens, a native of Pennsylvania and a graduate
of Jefferson College, was a leading figure in the organization
and development of the Episcopal church in Tennessee. After a long career as a teacher in Pennsylvania and Virginia,
he removed to Tennessee and became an Episcopal priest.
He and two other priests (there were only three Episcopal
clergymen in Tennessee at that time) assembled a convention in 1829, and in 1833 Bishop John Stark Ravenscroft of
North Carolina joined the three clergymen and organized
the diocese of Tennessee.

The newly recognized protestant churches in the South
soon learned that they could get aid from their Northern
brethren. The Yankee preachers had seen that the Southern
fields were white unto the harvest. Some of them were already at work, and many more would follow them in the
religious field. Shubal Stearns of Boston had joined the New
Lights, as the Congregational churches that followed George
Whitfield in New England were called. He soon joined the
Baptist church and was ordained in 1751. Anticipating
greater success in the ministry in the South than in Massa-

chusetts, Stearns moved to Virginia from whence, after a short period, he moved to Sandy Creek, North Carolina. There he gathered a band of sixteen followers and organized a church. Within a short time the parent body had added over six hundred members and had organized several new congregations. The congregations joined together to form the Sandy Creek Association. In less than twenty years the association had branches as far south as Georgia, east as the Atlantic, and north as the Chesapeake Bay. Forty-two churches had been organized, and they had sent out 125 ordained ministers. A contemporary, commenting on Stearns's work declared: "He managed to make soft impressions on the heart, bring tears from the eyes, and to shake the very nerves and throw the physical system into tumults and perturbations. And all the Separate Baptists copied after him."

Richard Furman, a regular Baptist minister, left New York in 1774 and moved to South Carolina where he was forbidden to preach because he was not a member of the established church. He supported William Tennent in the successful fight for the rights of dissenters in that state. Furman organized the First Baptist Church in Charleston, of which he was the pastor for thirty-seven years. He was a member of the South Carolina Baptist Convention and was president of the First Triennial Baptist Convention of 1814.

Many of the leaders in the establishment of the North Carolina Baptist Convention were Yankee ministers. Jesse Wait, a native of Vermont, proposed that such a body be formed in North Carolina. John Meredith, a native of Pennsylvania, wrote the constitution for the North Carolina Baptist Convention, Thomas Meredith, son of John, was elected the first president, and John Armstrong of Pennsylvania was appointed secretary of the convention. Thomas Meredith also established the *Biblical Recorder,* the official organ of the convention. Jesse Hartwell, a native of Massachusetts and a graduate of Brown University, served as president of the

Alabama State Baptist Convention, and James Barnett Tay-
lor of New York served as corresponding secretary of the
Southern Baptist Convention and established and edited the
Southern Baptist Missionary Journal.

Adiel Sherwood, a native of New York who was educated
at Union College and Andover Theological Seminary, was
one of the early Baptist leaders of Georgia, and he became
widely known for his contributions to the growth of the
Baptist church throughout the South and West. While at the
Andover Theological Seminary, Sherwood became a part-
time missionary and field representative of the Massachusetts Baptist Missionary Society. In 1818 he moved to Georgia and was ordained a Baptist minister in 1820. The
following year Sherwood traveled on horseback more than
three thousand miles, crisscrossing the state, and preached
330 sermons. He organized a score of churches and Sunday
schools, and established Bible and missionary societies all
over the state. He opened schools in the back country and
taught in academies in six different counties. In 1820 Sherwood wrote a resolution which he submitted to the separate
Baptist churches suggesting the organization of a state convention. The convention was organized in 1822, and Sherwood was elected secretary and treasurer, a post he held for
some years. Sherwood was the prime leader in getting the
Georgia State Convention to join the Baptist Triennial Convention in 1823, and he served as pastor of several of the
leading Baptist churches in the state. It was Sherwood who
proposed that the state convention set up a manual labor
school, which he in turn converted into Mercer University
in 1838, the leading Baptist university in Georgia. Sherwood
became professor of sacred literature in the university. He
later established and was president of the Marshall Baptist
College in Griffin, Georgia. Sherwood left Georgia in 1841
to become president of Shurtleff College in Illinois, but returned to Georgia in 1845. After the division of the Baptist
Triennial Convention over slavery and the organization of

the Southern Baptist Convention, Sherwood served for a time as secretary of the Baptist Missionary Society. He was for fifty years a regular and frequent contributor to Baptist periodicals. His articles covered such subjects as education, missions, and the general advancement of the Baptist church. He was the compiler of *A Gazetteer of the State of Georgia,* which has gone through five editions, the last published only recently, and *Notes on the New Testament.*

Among the early Yankee leaders of the Presbyterian church in Virginia were William Graham, Samuel Stanhope Smith, and John Blair Smith. All were natives of Pennsylvania, had studied or taught in Princeton University, and were early advocates of American independence. Graham and John Blair Smith served in the Revolutionary Army and Smith led a company of Hampden-Sydney students into battle. John Blair Smith was a leader of the revival movement in Virginia from 1789 to 1791 and was president of the Presbyterian General Assembly in 1798. Samuel Stanhope Smith, president of Princeton University from 1775 to 1812, is credited with offering the first course in chemistry and natural science in any American college. He wrote various books on religious subjects including *Lectures on the Evidence of Christian Religion* and *The Principles of Natural and Revealed Religion.* These three men were highly influential in the spread of the Presbyterian church in the South.

Edward McGready, a native of Pennsylvania who moved to North Carolina, stopped at Hampden-Sydney College where he heard John Blair Smith, a leading figure in the revival movement, preach. McGready was so aroused that he determined to become an evangelist. His preaching in North Carolina was characterized by vehement denunciation of sin and hypocrisy. His hearers became divided between ardent supporters and bitter opponents. From the latter he received threatening letters; one, written in blood, warned him to leave the community on peril of his life. In 1796 McGready moved to Kentucky where his preaching

stirred the people deeply and paved the way for the great
revival which swept the South and West in 1800. The services were characterized by great excitement and physical
demonstrations. Camp meetings lasted for weeks; the people
went into trances, danced the holy dance, and spoke in un-
known tongues; they ran, jumped, and performed many
strange and weird feats. Out of the revival came the Cumberland Presbyterian church which differed with the parent
church on the question of classical education as a prerequi-
site for ministerial ordination and on the renunciation of
parts of the Westminster Confession. McGready first cast his
lot with the new organization but later returned to the ortho-
dox wing of the church.

William Swan Plummer, a native of Pennsylvania and a
graduate of Washington College in Virginia, studied theology at Princeton University and became a Presbyterian minister. He organized the first Presbyterian church in Danville,
Virginia, and held pastorates in various towns in North Carolina and Virginia. In 1837 Plummer founded the *Watchman
of the South,* which he edited until 1845. He was influential
in establishing the School for Deaf, Dumb, and Blind in
Staunton, Virginia, in 1838. Plummer was a professor at the
Columbia, South Carolina, Theological Seminary, and was
the author of more than twenty books dealing with theology
and religion.

George Junkin, a native of Pennsylvania and a graduate
of Jefferson College, had a long career as teacher and administrator in Northern colleges before he moved to Washington
College in Virginia in 1848. Junkin served the college as
president until 1861. He was a moderate on the slavery issue
and published *The Integrity of Our National Union versus Abolitionism,* in which he took the position that believing masters
ought to be obeyed by their slaves and tolerated by the
church, not excommunicated. Junkin argued that scriptural
aggressive attacks on slavery would rivet more firmly the
chains on the slave. He maintained that slavery was consti-

tutional and attacks upon it looked toward a dissolution of
the Union. Junkin favored colonization of the slaves in Africa and claimed that "experiments had demonstrated the
easy practicability of universal emancipation."

When secession and Civil War came, Junkin spoke
out boldly in a lecture at the college. He maintained that the
Union preceded independence and that no state had ever
been sovereign. "The doctrine of State Rights or state sovereignty," he said, "outside the limits of state constitutions and
the lines of democracy found in the United States Constitution, is necessarily subversive of the national government."
A restive Pennsylvania student wrote "Lincoln Junkin" on
Dr. Junkin's door and raised a Palmetto flag. Junkin ordered
a servant to take it down. When the flag came down, Junkin
stepped up and, taking some matches out of his pocket, set
the flag on fire. While it flamed up, Junkin said, "So punish
all efforts to dissolve this glorious Union." The students then
raised a flag over Washington's statue. Junkin asked the
faculty if it was to remain. They replied, "Yes," and, "re-
fusing to teach classes under such conditions," Junkin resigned as president of the college.

The Methodist Episcopal church split asunder in 1844
over the slavery issue, and Methodist clergy from the Southern states withdrew and organized the Methodist Episcopal
church, South. Henry B. Bascom and Stephen Olin, both
Yankees, were among the seceders. Bascom, a native of Vermont, was born in 1796. He was licensed to preach by the
Ohio Methodist Conference in 1813. Even without a college
education, he had a phenomenal career. He was successively
chaplain to the United States Congress, president of Madison College in Pennsylvania, agent of the American Colonization Society, and president of Transylvania University.
As a delegate to the Convention of Southern Methodists
which assembled in Louisville, Kentucky, in 1845, he helped
to draft the constitution of the Methodist Episcopal church,
South. Bascom became editor of the *Southern Methodist Quarter-*

ly Review in 1845, and wrote the book *Methodism and Slavery,* in which he upheld the Southern Methodist views on slavery. In 1850 he was elected a bishop of the Methodist Episcopal church, South.

Stephen Olin was born in Connecticut in 1797 and was graduated from Middlebury College in 1820. Olin moved to South Carolina, where he taught in an academy and renewed friendship with some college classmates. There he first became acquainted with the institution of slavery and seemed to accept it without criticism. In fact he became somewhat defensive of slavery when his Northern friends questioned him about it. Olin wrote: "I am much reconciled to Southern life. The little invectives in which my Northern friends sometimes indulge wound me almost as if I had been born in Carolina." Olin soon accepted a professorship at the University of Georgia which he held from 1826 to 1833. In the meantime he had studied for the ministry and was ordained an elder in the Methodist Episcopal church in 1833. Shortly thereafter Olin was elected president of Randolph-Macon, a Methodist college in Virginia. While there he began to publish articles in Methodist periodicals in which he urged the Methodist church to establish theological schools. They were, Olin wrote, "not only desirable but indispensable" for training ministers. "Nothing can save us but an able ministry and this cannot be had but through education." In 1842 he was elected president of Wesleyan University in Connecticut.

Olin was a delegate from New York to the General Conference of the Methodist Episcopal church and was appointed a member of the committee whose purpose was to find a basis of agreement between the proslavery South and the antislavery North. He had had long experience with slavery while teaching in the South and expressed his views honestly and forthrightly. He wrote in his diary as follows: I have "a deep feeling of apprehension that the difficulties that are upon us now threaten to be unmanageable. . . . I do not see how Northern men can yield their ground, or Southern men give up theirs . . . if Southern men concede that holding slaves is incompatible with holding their ministry—they may as well go to the Rocky Mountains as to their own plains. The people would not hear it." Olin believed that the South had the church law and constitution on its side, and he took the position that the demand of Northern Methodists that the Southern Methodists give up their slaves was neither judicial nor punitive and could not be enforced. Therefore he held himself aloof from the controversy.

Samuel Gilman, a native of Massachusetts and a graduate of Harvard College, might be considered a spokesman of the Unitarian church in the South. He moved to Charleston, South Carolina, in 1819 and resided there until his death in 1858. A man of liberal views, Gilman was a leader in the religious, cultural, and social life of Charleston and moved easily back and forth between Charleston and Boston. He was a writer of poetry and prose, both of which he contributed to the *North American Review* and he published a volume entitled *Contributions to Literature*. In an address published in 1831 Gilman spoke out boldly against the use of strong drink, urging "strict and entire abstinence from ardent spirits." In another address on Unitarian Christianity he emphasized "freedom of thought and inquiry" for all people on all issues. He was, however, actually making a plea for freedom of the Unitarians. Gilman is probably best known today for his *Fair Harvard.*

John Backman, a minister and scientist, was one of the great men of America during the first half of the nineteenth century. He was born in Rhinebeck, New York, in 1790 and died in Columbia, South Carolina, in 1874. He attended Williams College, studied theology under the Reverend Philip M. Mayer, and was licensed a Lutheran minister in 1813. He moved to South Carolina in 1815 and became the pastor of St. Johns Lutheran Church, a post he held until his death. Backman welcomed Negroes to his church although

they were seated in a gallery and took communion separate
from the whites. Backman rapidly expanded the area of his
church activities: in 1824 he organized a Lutheran synod
with congregations he had formed in Georgia and South
Carolina; in 1828 he established a female academy which in
1860 had 150 students; in 1834 he established a theological
seminary and a classical school; and in 1856 he founded
Newberry College. In selecting professors for the latter institution Backman took care to see that they were not only
"sound in learning but also attached to the peculiar institution of our Southern States." It is of interest to note that his
father was a slaveholder in New York.

Backman's deep and abiding interest was in the natural
sciences, and in this field he made his fame and enduring
reputation. He once recalled, "From my earliest childhood
I had an irrepressible desire for the study of natural history."
His study and experimentation in plant life led to the organization of the Horticultural Society of South Carolina in
1833. Backman and John James Audubon were drawn together through their interest in bird and animal life and the
marriage of two of Backman's daughters to two of Audubon's
sons. The two scientists cooperated in *Birds of America* and the
Viviparous Quadrupeds of North America in three volumes. Backman seemed to be more concerned about the accuracy of
these works than Audubon. The latter wished to include a
"blue-headed Pigeon" as a Florida species. But Backman
wrote urging him not to do so. He said: "As you did not kill
any of the birds, you might have been mistaken—your reputation [for accuracy] is worth more than a dozen of new
species." Backman wrote the text for the *Quadrupeds of America*. This work brought him great fame and reputation. Jean
Louis Agassiz said the work had no equal in America. Backman was awarded several honorary degrees for his scientific
work, one of which was the doctor of philosophy degree from
the University of Berlin.

In the mid-nineteenth century scientists became involved

in the controversy over the biblical story of creation and the scientific theory of evolution. In his work *Unity of the Human Race*, published in 1850, Backman took the position that all men were of one species, thus foreshadowing Darwin's view in his *Origin of Species*. What Backman was trying to do, however, was to reconcile science with the Bible. His work *Experiments on the Vulture* is one that exhibits the *absolute* in scientific interest and research. He captured a vulture feeding on carrion, forced it to disgorge, and then tested the food in an effort to study the human digestive process.

In his later years Backman became a violent and outspoken sectionalist and champion of slavery and Southern rights. In the South Carolina nullification crisis of the 1830s Backman had expressed "deepest convictions" in support of the Unionist cause, but by 1851 he had become an "ardent supporter of separation from the Federal Union." Backman wrote his son-in-law Victor G. Audubon on September 1, 1851, that he was "growing every day less attached to the Union & if South Carolina declares for secession I will for weal or woe go with her. If we are not to speak as equals in the Union I would rather preserve my independence with a crust of bread & be out of it." On January 30, 1857, again writing to his son-in-law, Backman said: "I think the days of the Union are nearly numbered. The black republicans are fast rising into power—when they do, the South will walk out of the Union—peacefully if she can forcibly if she must—I shall sink or swim with the Southern Ship." In a sermon delivered on November 11, 1860, he enjoined on his people the necessity of firmness, dignity, and moderation at a time when secession was inevitable. "Truth and justice," he said, "are on our side let us do our duty as men and citizens, and all will be well." Division, he declared, was a melancholy thought, but it was better to separate since the North and South could no longer live together in peace. During the war he worked for the Soldier's Relief Association, and he collected money and supplies for the Confederate troops. He was given what was termed "barbarous treatment . . . [by] the Federal troops who insisted that he knew the whereabouts of hidden gold and silver." But worst of all, he said "My whole library and my collections in Natural History, the accumulation of the labor of a long life, were burnt by Sherman's vandal army." His great joy was that one of Humboldt's letters was saved. Thus closed the life of a Yankee preacher and scientist who had become one of the South's most distinguished sons. As has been said, "Men make history. Their ideas and their hopes, their goals and contrivances for reaching those goals, shape all experience, past and present."

New England Yankees played a significant role in their efforts to educate, civilize, and Christianize the Indian tribes who made their home in the Old South. Cyrus King of New Hampshire, an advance agent of the American Missionary Board, blazed the trail for a large number of men and women who devoted their talents and lives to this undertaking. A graduate of Brown University and Andover Theological Seminary, King was sent in 1815 by the American Missionary Board to study the habits of the Cherokee tribe, and thus he was given the opportunity for mission work among them. He attended a council with the Indians, won their confidence, and purchased lands in Tennessee upon which the Brainard Mission was established. In 1818 he traveled four hundred miles by wagon into Mississippi and established a mission in that state. Later when the five civilized tribes were removed by the United States government to the lands west of the Mississippi River, King spent five months in the region and chose Pine Ridge for the new mission in Indian territory. There he made his home until his death in 1870. His work, as an agent of the American Missionary Board, has been characterized as the most influential of any in the Cherokee Nation.

King was followed by scores of Yankee missionaries who carried on the work at Brainard in Tennessee and New

Echota in Georgia. A large number of the missionaries were graduates of Union, Middlebury, Dartmouth, Princeton, or other New England colleges, and they established numerous missions in the Southern states. The missionaries were accompanied by New England teachers, blacksmiths, physicians, millwrights, mechanics, carpenters, cobblers and farmers. Two examples will suffice. Gideon Blackburn was superintendent of a Mission School at which some four hundred children were taught to read and write the English language. Ainsworth Emory Blunt, a native of New Hampshire, was trained as a teacher, but he also supervised the training of farmers and mechanics. He accompanied, as did many other missionaries, the Cherokees on their "Trail of Tears" to Oklahoma. He later returned to Brainard, purchased the land, and was caretaker of the cemetery.

Three of the missionaries, John Thompson, Elihu Butler, and Samuel Austin Worcester, were principals in a significant controversy between the state of Georgia and the United States as to which had authority over the people in the Indian missions. Thompson, a native of New York and a graduate of Middlebury College, had studied theology at Princeton University. He was arrested in 1831 for residing in the Cherokee Nation without a permit required by the state of Georgia. He was discharged by Judge Augustin A. Clayton with the understanding that he would leave the state. Failing to do so Thompson was again arrested, tried, convicted, and confined in the state prison at Milledgeville. Butler, a native of Connecticut and a licensed physician, had followed his profession among the Indians since 1821. He, too, was arrested in 1831, tried, and imprisoned. After his release in 1834, he accompanied the Cherokees to the Indian territory as their physician. He settled at Fairfield where he practiced his profession until 1850, at which time he was appointed steward of the Cherokee Female Academy. Worcester, born in Vermont in 1798, was a graduate of the University of Vermont and the Andover Theological Seminary. Ordained in the Congregational Church of Boston, he was sent to the Brainard Mission in 1825. He soon moved to New Echota, Georgia, where he aided in establishing the *Cherokee Phoenix* and translated and published the Bible in the Cherokee language. On July 7, 1831, he was arrested, tried, convicted, and imprisoned for violating the Georgia law. He appealed to the United States Supreme Court, which in *Worcester* v. *Georgia* declared the Georgia law unconstitutional. Released from prison, Worcester removed to the Indian territory where he established the Park Hill Mission. There he organized the Cherokee Bible Society, established the first printing press in the territory in 1838, and published the *Cherokee Almanac* until his death in 1859.

The religious press of the Old South was not only important to the individual denominations but was also significant in the dissemination of news and views of the life and times of the period. Nearly every religious sect had an official journal, and there were many unofficial periodicals of note. A large number of the editors were Northern born and educated, but nearly all of them were intensely loyal to the South and supported the institution of slavery.

Joseph L. Walker, a native of Pennsylvania, moved to Virginia as a youth and was educated at the University of Virginia and the Virginia Baptist Seminary. He was a vigorous proponent of missionary work, an ardent supporter of education, and a champion of slavery. He was positive and forthright in expressing his views as an editor and often became involved in arguments with his readers. While editing the *Baptist Recorder* in Virginia from 1847 to 1850, he wrote that he had "stirred up a first class hornet's nest [by one of his editorials] which made it necessary for the editor to preach a three hour sermon on baptism . . . and to debate for four hours with [another minister] on the same subject." For a time he edited the *Christian Index* but resigned because the publication committee would not increase his pay. He then established and edited the *Baptist Champion* in Macon,

Georgia, in 1859 and 1860, but closed it down in the interest of denominational harmony.

Thomas Meredith, a native of Pennsylvania and a graduate of the university of that state, was sent by the Baptist General Convention as a missionary to North Carolina in 1818. He settled permanently in the state and came to be recognized as one of the ablest Baptist preachers in North Carolina. He founded the *Biblical Recorder and Southern Workman* in New Bern, North Carolina, which was moved to Raleigh and as the *Biblical Recorder* is still the official organ of the North Carolina Baptist State Convention. John W. Tobey, a native of Rhode Island and a graduate of Columbian University in Washington, D.C., was editor of the *Recorder* from 1850 to 1853. He later became a missionary in China.

Milo Parker Jewett, a native of Vermont and a graduate of Dartmouth, who founded Judson College in Alabama and was its president from 1838 to 1855, was editor of the *Alabama Baptist,* the official organ of the Alabama Baptist State Convention for a number of years.

The Presbyterian church in the South also had a number of distinguished editors of both official and independent journals. William Swan Plummer, a native of Pennsylvania and a graduate of Washington College in Virginia and of the Princeton Theological Seminary, was pastor of the First Presbyterian Church in Richmond from 1837 to 1845. He founded and edited the *Watchman of the South,* absorbed three other Presbyterian periodicals of the old school, and built up what was said to be the largest circulation of any political or religious journal in Virginia.

Benjamin Gildersleeve, a native of Connecticut and a graduate of Princeton, was undoubtedly the most influential of the editors of church periodicals in the Old South. For more than half a century he was an outstanding teacher, minister, and journalist. He began his teaching at Mount Zion Academy in Georgia in 1819. He established the *Missionary,* a nonsectarian journal in which he reported activities of charitable societies, Baptist associations, Methodist conferences, and Presbyterian synods. He then became editor of the *Georgia Reporter and Christian Index* in Sparta, Georgia. Moving to Charleston, South Carolina, in 1827, Gildersleeve established the Charleston *Observer* and absorbed Benjamin M. Palmer's *Southern Evangelical Intelligencer* which had been established in 1819. The *Observer* soon became the South's largest and most influential Presbyterian journal. Gildersleeve moved the *Observer* to Richmond and continued publication under the name *Central Presbyterian*. On January 5, 1856, Gildersleeve stated his views on the serious sectional conflict: "In the threatening aspect of Political affairs, and the period . . . that now menaces the permanence of our Federal Union, it is very important that we should have an organ of communication with our people, that will be under our control, watchful of our interests, and faithful to those great *conservative* principles that underlie all our institutions. Our political and geographic position, central between the extreme North and extreme South, creates peculiar responsibilities and duties. . . . We have in our colored population an interest that God has trusted specially to our charge." Gildersleeve filled the magazine with religious, secular, and political affairs, as well as sermons, poems, and essays of all kinds. But he was always alert to the tension between the North and South. It is little wonder that his famous son Basil L. Gildersleeve, who held degrees from Princeton and Göttingen universities and was a professor of Greek at the University of Virginia in 1861, shortly offered his services to the Confederacy and served in the army until wounds forced his retirement. After the war he published his famous essay *The Creed of the Old South*.

FIVE

Agriculturalists and Industrialists

THE AGRICULTURAL PATTERN OF THE OLD SOUTH HAD
been fixed during the colonial era. Tobacco became the
major staple crop for Virginia and Maryland, and tobacco
growing spread into North Carolina, South Carolina, and
Georgia to a lesser degree. Rice and indigo were introduced
into South Carolina and spread into North Carolina and
Georgia. These three staple crops were supplemented by
wheat and livestock in all the Southern colonies. Cultivation
of the staple crops required a large labor force and resulted
in the introduction of Negro slaves. By far the larger part of
the Southern people were subsistence farmers and raised few
staples for sale, and many of the lower-class whites eked out
a bare existence.

The American Revolution disrupted the Southern agricultural pattern. The upper Southern states turned more
and more to wheat and livestock in the western section, while
the lower Southern states sought and found a new staple to
replace indigo that had ceased to be profitable. This new
staple was the black seed, long-staple cotton grown successfully only in South Carolina and Georgia. Great profits were
derived from this new staple, but its area of cultivation was
limited mainly to the sea islands and a narrow coastal strip.
The green seed, short-staple cotton could be grown widely
throughout the Carolinas and Georgia and to a lesser degree
in Virginia, but the labor required to handpick the seed from

the lint made its cultivation unprofitable. This situation led mechanics to look for a machine that would do the job. William Longstreet, a native of New Jersey who had removed to Augusta, Georgia, in 1785 turned his attention to this problem, and he built and patented a gin for removing the seed from the green seed cotton. But, unfortunately, it crushed the seed and the oil ruined the lint. A Massachusetts Yankee was to succeed where Longstreet had failed. Eli Whitney, a tutor in the home of Gen. Nathaniel Greene near Augusta, Georgia, in 1793 built a gin with which one laborer could clean fifty pounds of lint cotton per day. He received a patent for his gin and in 1794 began the manufacture of cotton gins, and cotton became the great staple. It suffered somewhat during the stormy period of the controversy between the United States and England and the war of 1812, but it soon recovered and the yield rose steadily, doubling each decade except that of the 1840s, until 1860. King Cotton was to reign throughout the Southern states from North Carolina to Texas until well into the twentieth century.

Another staple crop, sugarcane, was added with the purchase of Louisiana in 1803. For many years the sugar planters were both agriculturalists and manufacturers. The planters ground the cane, manufactured sugar at mills on their own plantations, and were able to build up a considerable estate in a relatively short period. For instance, Andrew McCollam moved from New York to Donaldson, Louisiana, in 1838. He worked as a surveyor until 1843, when he bought a run-down sugar plantation. He went to work to improve the plantation; he constructed farm buildings, a smokehouse, and a sugar mill. He entered into a partnership with a planter who supplied the slave labor force for a portion of the profits. In 1850 McCollam sold his interest in the plantation for $30,000, almost double the cost of the entire plantation in 1843. In 1851 McCollam bought another plantation for $50,000. By 1860 he had paid for the plantation which was then valued at $150,000 and owned a labor force of eighty-seven slaves. McCollam was a Union Whig, and after Abraham Lincoln was elected president in 1860, McCollam urged that the Southern states remain in the Union until Lincoln should "commit some overt act." He said that "South Carolina had always been a 'damphool' State, and deserved to be whipped into the traces." As a member of the Louisiana Secession Convention in 1861 McCollam signed the state's secession ordinance, but he wrote his wife that signing the ordinance was "the bitterest pill" he had ever taken. After the Civil War McCollam played an active role in the establishment of the Louisiana Sugar Planters' Association.

The bitter controversy over slavery and abolition in the 1820s and 1830s that did so much to develop Southern sectionalism and nationalism coincided in time with grave political problems, including tariff, nullification, the removal of the Southern Indian tribes, and a serious economic depression. The older and upper South felt the economic pinch in the twenties and thirties, the newer and lower South in the thirties and forties. Declining prices of staple crops, currency dislocation, and the Panic of 1837, which did not subside until the mid-forties, caused Southern leaders to calculate the value of the Union and to study their own position. They proposed measures designed to restore economic prosperity and to break their economic dependence on Northern factors, merchants, bankers, and shippers. These efforts helped to bring on what historians have called an agricultural and industrial revolution in the South; and the 1850s was the most prosperous decade experienced by the Old South. Furthermore the South suffered less from the Panic of 1857 than did the North.

The Southern Yankee played an important role in this agricultural and industrial development. Nearly all Yankees were ignorant of staple crop agriculture when they first came to the South, and they were inclined to look askance at slave labor. Most of them, however, soon accepted the idea that agriculture was the foundation stone of Southern economy and that Negro slaves constituted the chief source of labor. Consequently, many Southern Yankees turned to agriculture for their livelihood. As they prospered, they bought slaves and began to cultivate staple crops, and some of them became large slaveholding planters. In addition wealthy Yankee merchants, shippers, and industrialists bought well-stocked plantations and joined the planter social group. Other Yankees married wealthy heiresses and moved immediately into upper-class society.

In 1840 a colony of 120 New York Yankee families purchased 24,000 acres of land near Alexandria, Virginia, for $180,000. Among them was a former member of the Congress of the United States. Some of this land had been owned by Richard Bland Lee. The land had been worn out by successive cropping and lack of manuring, and the former owner had moved with his slaves to new lands in the Southwest. The Yankee purchasers moved in and began a program of improvement. They followed a system of deep plowing, crop rotation, sowing clover and other cover crops, and the use of new and improved farm tools and implements. They also introduced fine cattle and horses and Southdown sheep. Some of the new owners brought hired laborers from New York; others hired local laborers, both whites and free Negroes. A reporter of the Richmond *Whig* told the story of the colony in 1845. He attributed much of the improvement "to the enterprise and industry" of the Yankees. "Here [he said] are fields which a few years ago were thrown out as . . . [exhausted. They are now] covered with luxuriant vegetation, the barnyards supplied with handsome and well fed stock . . . and the neat and tasteful dwellings furnished with all the comforts of life." He also said that under these conditions "labor was rendered respectable." In closing he said: "It is pleasing to observe that a spirit of improvement has seized upon other minds in the vicinity and new life and activity has been infused into the community around them."

Thomas Green Clemson, a Pennsylvania Yankee, was lured to the South by marriage. His wife was the former Anna Maria Calhoun, daughter of John C. Calhoun. Clemson was educated at the Sorbonne, where he was trained in chemistry and mining engineering. He was a consultant in engineering and the developer of the La Motte Iron Mine in Missouri. Clemson moved to South Carolina in 1840 where he managed Calhoun's Fort Hill Plantation and purchased Canebrake Plantation for himself. He also managed Calhoun's gold mines in Dahlonega, Georgia. Clemson was chargé d'affaires in Belgium from 1844 to 1851 where he negotiated a commercial treaty and also worked to promote direct trade between Belgium and the Southern states. During the 1850s Clemson devoted much time to the study of and writing on agricultural and technical education, and he was influential in the founding of the Maryland College of Agriculture. In February of 1860, Jacob Thompson, secretary of the interior, appointed Clemson superintendent of agricultural affairs and authorized him to go to Europe to get seeds and plants of various sorts and to establish a greenhouse under the supervision of the department. The work was cut short by the secession of South Carolina in 1860. Clemson was opposed to secession but followed his adopted state and entered the Confederate Army in 1861. He supervised the Nitre and Mining Corps until 1863 when he was transferred to the Trans-Mississippi Department. There he was engaged in iron manufacturing. Clemson spent his last years at Fort Hill Plantation where he raised funds with which to establish "an institution for the diffusion of scientific knowledge so that we may once more become a happy and prosperous people." In his will he left his property for a college now known as Clemson University.

A remarkable group of Yankee agricultural reformers and horticulturalists appeared in Georgia during the 1840s and 1850s. Among the more distinguished and successful were Richard Peters; Robert Nelson; Jarvis Van Buren; and

Louis E. and Jules Prosper Berckman, father and son. Peters,
son of a Pennsylvania agriculturalist and businessman,
moved to Georgia as an assistant engineer on the Georgia
Railroad in 1835. He surveyed a line for a road to Mobile,
Alabama, and later became superintendent of the Georgia
Railroad. He introduced such improvements as headlights
and spark arresters on the wood-burning engines, and he
provided crude sleeping car accommodations on the train
long before the Pullman car was invented. Peters was director of the Atlanta and West Point and president of the Georgia Western Railroad. While on a hunting expedition in
Gordon County he observed that the land was very similar
to that in his home community in Pennsylvania, and he
bought fifteen hundred acres of land, acquired a slave labor
force, and developed the plantation into a model one. Peters
experimented with new crops for that region. These included
sorghum cane, millet, and more than twenty grasses including Bermuda, orchard grass, red and white clover, alfalfa,
and oat grass. He also went in heavily for livestock breed-
ing—horses; cattle, including Alderney, Guernsey, Jersey,
Durham, Devon, and Brahman; hogs; sheep; poultry; and
goats. He was the first to introduce the Angora goat into the
United States, and he bred and shipped them to states as far
away as Texas. He won national recognition as a breeder of
livestock and took prizes at many state fairs and livestock
shows. He sold and shipped stock as far north as North
Carolina and as far west as California and to various states
between. Peters also engaged in fruit culture. He had a
nursery and shipped seeds and plants into several states. One
Georgia historian has said, "For forty years Peters led all
Georgians in scientific and advanced farming." Martin W.
Philips, the noted Mississippi agriculturalist, said that
"Richard Peters was doing more for his region than any
other Southerner." Peters entered the milling industry and
in 1856 owned the largest flour mill south of Richmond,
Virginia. Peters was opposed to secession but was loyal to the

Confederacy. During the Civil War he engaged in blockade running, bringing in supplies for the Confederacy, and organized Atlanta's first street railway system.

In 1854 Peters joined with two other Yankees, Dennis Redmond and Robert Battey, and introduced Chinese sorghum cane into Georgia. Redmond, editor of the *Southern Cultivator,* secured a few seeds from an "enterprising firm in Boston" in 1854. That firm had bought the seed in France where it had been imported from China in 1851. Redmond gave some seed to Richard Peters and Jarvis Van Buren. The new plant was variously called sorgo sucre or Chinese sugarcane. Redmond pointed out that the cane had not yet been grown in the United States but that he believed it "would succeed well in the Southern States, and deserved to be tested, if only for fodder." He urged experimentation with the cane on the ground that syrup and sugar might be made of it, that it would make good feed for livestock, and that the bagasse might be useful for commercial usage, papermaking for instance.

Richard Peters planted the seed, and in 1856 the wife of his overseer boiled the juice from the cane and made syrup. Peters immediately decided to install equipment and manufacture syrup for commercial purposes. He called on Robert Battey, a friend and chemist who had come to Georgia from Pennsylvania, to aid him. Battey scientifically prepared the juice, added various ingredients for clarifying the liquid, boiled the juice, and found that the syrup was edible. Redmond then prepared a pamphlet to inform the farmers and planters of the possibilities of the new food crop. The Georgia piedmont region produced a high yield of cane and the syrup could be easily manufactured by the farmer, as well as the planter. Many whites did not like the syrup at first but "sorghum sirip," or molasses as it was often called, became a part of the basic diet of Negro slaves and most of the poor white farmers as well.

Robert Nelson, a native of Denmark, came to the United

States and settled in New York. He was a graduate of a
European university and had been a horticulturalist and
nurseryman in Europe. He moved from New York to Augusta, Georgia, in 1840 where he established a nursery but soon
moved to Macon. He was a founder of the Central Horticultural Association organized in Macon in 1849, and he edited
the horticultural department of the Macon *Georgia Citizen.* In
1852, Nelson established the Troup Hill Nursery near Macon. He wrote that if his horticultural experience over a
period of thirty-eight years should be of service to his adopted country he would happily give the public the results of his
studies. He urged gardeners to use ashes, leaves, stable ma-
nure, and all sorts of fertilizer, and make a compost heap for
flowers and shrubs. Noah B. Cloud wrote that "Nelson's
name and reputation as an experienced Horticulturalist are
well known in this country among fruit growers, and as
familiar as household words." But it was Nelson's work with
peaches that was to make him famous. He criticized Northern nursery stock and insisted that "grafting from parent
stock in order to produce uniform fruit" was preferable. He
maintained that the South had every advantage over the
North in commercial peach growing and would eventually
supply the Northern market. Noting that Northern peaches
were brought to Southern ports in September and October,
Nelson asked: "Why don't we raise such peaches at home?
Why don't we make the tide roll back by sending our early
varieties to Northern markets?" Nelson's encouragement
contributed greatly to the development of peach culture in
Georgia, and numerous commercial orchards were established in the 1850s. The Augusta *Constitutionalist* in 1858 reported nine cars of peaches shipped in one day from Macon
to Savannah and thence by steamer to New York. And the
New York *Tribune* in 1858 reported that "Georgia growers found peaches a very profitable fruit for shipment to New
York and large orchards are cultivated on the railroads leading . . . to Savannah . . . for the supply of the New York

Market." The price range that season was from three dollars to fifteen dollars per bushel. Nelson's efforts had begun to bear fruit in more ways than one.

Jarvis Van Buren, a New York Yankee who moved to Georgia in 1840, did for the apple what Robert Nelson had done for the peach. Van Buren had grown up in the Mohawk Valley apple-growing region of New York, and he recognized the possibilities of an apple culture in Habersham County, Georgia, where he had settled. There he established the Glooming Nursery and began a study of the local apples. He contributed articles to the *Southern Cultivator* and other periodicals on the importance of developing the native apples. Van Buren noted that Andrew Jackson Downing listed only one Georgia apple in his *Fruit and Fruit Trees of America*. Van Buren urged that some organization should name the state's fruit trees, whereupon the South Carolina Agricultural Society employed him to tour the region and identify and classify the fruit trees. He "made full sized drawings and colored them with remarkable fidelity, thus beginning a system of nomenclature of native fruits." In general Van Buren chose place names for the apples—for example, the Mountain Belle, Nantahala, Green Mountain Pippin. Having named the apples, Van Buren set out to convince the people that Georgia could produce superior apples. In 1854 he sent Georgia apples to the Lancaster, Pennsylvania, County Fair. He received a report that "taking all the good qualities of these Southern seedlings . . . that an equal number could not be made in Lancaster County . . . at all comparable to them." Van Buren voiced the view that in the future "the North must pay back the amount she has received from the South with interest for fruit and fruit trees [we have] purchased from her." Pomology grew rapidly in the decade of the 1850s. Apples in northern Georgia, where cotton did not grow, became a staple crop. Today a huge concrete red apple is the hallmark of Clarksville, Georgia, where Van Buren labored a hundred years ago. The Byrd family of Virginia and apple growers of other Southern states have developed and expanded Van Buren's initial project.

Charles Albert Peabody was born in Connecticut in 1810, moved to Georgia in 1834, and shortly thereafter moved to Alabama where he became "one of the best known exponents of gardening in the South." An uncle of the great philanthropist of the same name, Peabody had a limited education but he was an "avid reader and had an insatiable thirst for beauty and culture." When he moved to Columbus, Georgia, he was a tailor by trade; but a transient clientele, poor collections, and a disastrous fire put him out of business, and he removed to Russell County, Alabama. There he bought a farm, built a log house, and beset by "a great passion for agriculture, he began to work on his farm." He was a successful farmer and became a slaveholder. Peabody was the editor of two agricultural journals, *Soil of the South* and the *American Cotton Planter*. But strawberry culture was his greatest interest. He studied it as a science and was called by the agricultural journals of his day, "the most successful strawberry culturalist in the world." In 1841 Peabody began a study to develop a strawberry suitable for the South. He ordered seedlings from Hovey's New York Nursery but found that while they bloomed they bore no fruit. By scientific study and experimentation in pollination he discovered that there was no fertilization. He then crossed Hovey's plants with the local Early Scarlet variety and was able to get a yield of some two hundred bushels per acre. Calling his new variety the Peabody seedling, Peabody shipped his berries to the largest markets in the United States. Nicholas Longsworth, the leading strawberry culturist in Cincinnati, Ohio, curious as to Peabody's secret, asked the Cincinnati Horticultural Society to make a study of pollination. The report was made in 1846 and confirmed Peabody's findings; he now lost some of his Northern market. But the Peabody strawberry remained for decades one of the most important berries in the lower South.

Thomas Affleck, a Scotsman who resided in New York and Ohio for ten years before he moved to Mississippi in 1842, became a noted planter, nurseryman, and agricultural publicist in the Gulf Coast area. He bought a plantation near Washington, Mississippi, where he developed an experimental farm and a Southern nursery. Some years later he established a branch of his Southern nursery in Texas. He edited and published the *Southern Agricultural Almanac* and *Plantation Gardens*. Affleck's nurseries supplied seeds and plants to farmers throughout the Southwest, and his almanacs served as guides for planting, cultivating, pruning, and harvesting of fruits. But his most important work was the *Plantation Book* first published in 1847 and reprinted many times over. The *Book*, as it was generally called, was widely used throughout the South. The number of copies printed in 1853 was 3,397. Many planters made it a part of their contracts with overseers that "the *Books* were to be carefully kept and returned at the end of the year." The *Book* brought sound and uniform record keeping, and factors had no hesitation in making advances on crops provided the *Plantation Book* was presented for their scrutiny and was found satisfactory. In fact, the "*Plantation Book* was accepted as evidence by the courts as freely as the entry in a merchant clerk's *Day Book*." Solon Robinson, a Connecticut Yankee who moved to the West and became known as one of the leading agricultural reformers of the United States, said, "Plantations in the area under the influence of Thomas Affleck and other such reformers bore the appearance of a well ordered No. 1 Yankee farm."

Many of the Yankees who went to Texas became ranchers, cattlemen, and sheepmen. Richard King, a native of New York, ran away from home as a teen-age boy and worked his way to Texas via Florida and Alabama. He fought in the Seminole War in Florida, moved to Mobile, and worked on a steamboat plying up and down the rivers which flow into Mobile Bay. From Mobile he moved to Texas where he bought a steamboat and engaged in trade on the Rio Grande. He organized a company, which built or purchased twenty-two steamers, and engaged in the cotton trade with Mexico and California in which he made a considerable fortune. In 1852 he acquired seventy-five thousand acres of land and established the King Ranch. He slaughtered cattle, engaged in the long drives to market, and entered the beef, tallow, and hides industry. His ranch was not limited to cattle of which he had a herd of one hundred thousand; he also owned twenty thousand sheep and ten thousand horses. At his death in 1885 he owned more than five hundred thousand acres of land.

Edward Hopkins Cushing, a native of Vermont and a graduate of Dartmouth College, moved to Galveston, Texas, where he taught school for a short time. He then moved to Columbia where he edited and published the *Democrat and Planter*. In 1856 he moved to Houston where he founded and edited the *Telegraph* in which he advocated the building of railroads. He was a vigorous proponent of "a university in Texas equal to any in the United States and at which all, rich and poor, [could] have the means of an education unsurpassed anywhere." He also called for a "first rate library, . . . a first rate astronomical laboratory," and "full scholarships" for "at least forty or fifty students." Cushing built a nursery and introduced into the state artichokes, celery, asparagus, cauliflower, and other vegetables. He had a regular staff correspondent on the *Telegraph* to report developments in scientific agriculture. Cushing accepted the Southern position on slavery, supported the South when secession came, and served as an officer in the Confederate Army.

The predominance of agriculture in the Old South and the dependence of the South on the North for manufactured goods had been a factor in the economic depression in the South in the 1830s and 1840s. Hence in seeking to improve their economic situation, Southern leaders directed attention to the development of manufactures of various sorts. Among those who spoke and wrote to arouse the people none was more forthright and outspoken than Albert Pike, a native of Boston with a degree from Harvard University, who settled in Little Rock, Arkansas, in 1835. Pike, a poet of some repute, edited the *Arkansas Gazette,* was a reporter for the Arkansas Supreme Court, served in the Mexican War, was commissioned by the Confederacy to negotiate treaties of alliance with the Southwest Indian tribes, and was a brigadier general in the Confederate Army. Speaking before a Southern Commercial Convention in New Orleans in 1850, Pike said: "From the rattle with which the nurse tickles the ear of the child born in the South to the shroud which covers the cold form of the dead, everything comes to us from the North. We rise from between sheets made in Northern looms, and pillows of Northern feathers, to wash in basins made in the North, dry our beards on Northern towels, and dress ourselves in garments made in Northern looms; we eat from Northern plates and dishes; our rooms are swept with Northern brooms, our gardens are dug with Northern spades, and our bread kneaded in trays or dishes of Northern wood or tin; and the very wood which feeds our fires is cut with Northern axes, helved with hickory brought from Connecticut or New York; and when we die our bodies are wrapped in shrouds manufactured in New England, put in coffins made in the North. We have our graves filled with Southern soil but it is pulled in by Northern spades and shovels."

Frederick A. P. Barnard, one of the great Yankee educators of the Old South, also prodded the South to free itself of the Northern economic yoke. In a Fourth of July address in 1851 he said: "At present, the North fattens and grows rich upon the South. We depend upon it for our entire supplies. We purchase all our luxuries and necessities from the North. . . . With us, every branch and pursuit in life, every trade, profession and occupation is dependent upon the North; for instance, the Northerners abuse and denounce

slavery and slaveholders, yet our slaves are clothed with
Northern manufactured goods, have Northern hats and
shoes, work with Northern hoes, ploughs, and other imple-
ments, are chastised with Northern made whips, and are
working for Northern more than Southern profit." Thus far
Barnard's argument was nearly identical with that of Pike,
but Barnard also tied the industrial argument to the agricultural system. He pointed out that Southern Negro slaves
were fed with Northern bacon, beef, and flour; and he urged
planters to grow grain and livestock. These claims, however,
were not original with the Southern Yankees. Hinton Rowan
Helper, a native of North Carolina, had used much the same
argument in his *Impending Crisis of the South, and How to Meet
It.* What is significant, however, was that the Yankees had
become Southerners and were urging Southerners to free
themselves from Northern economic bondage.

The role of Pike and Barnard, and other Yankees who
agreed with them, was to arouse native Southerners to action, but there were many Yankees who contributed directly
to industrial development in the South. Daniel Pratt of Temple, New Hampshire, with only nine months of schooling, a
bundle of clothes slung over his shoulder, and twenty-five
dollars in his pocket, arrived in Georgia in 1819 ready to seek
his fortune. He found employment in the Samuel Griswold
Cotton Gin Factory, but after a short sojourn moved on to
Alabama and established his own gin factory at what was to
become Prattville, Alabama. Pratt enjoyed phenomenal success, and in a few years was manufacturing between 750 and
1,000 gins per year. He soon expanded his business and built
a textile factory, a woolen mill, sawmill, shingle mill, sash-
blind-and-door factory, flour mill, gristmill, a limekiln, brick
factory, marble works, blacksmith shop, tinworks, foundry,
carriage and wagon factory, and a boot and shoe factory.
Pratt also invested in and helped to build railroads. Having
grown wealthy from his industrial enterprises, he bought
land, slaves, and livestock and became a planter. He gave

freely to those who were less successful and built a school, two churches, a print shop, and an art museum for which he acquired works of leading artists. A Whig in politics, Pratt was elected to the state legislature. He supported John Bell of Tennessee, the Constitutional Union candidate for president in 1860. He opposed secession but supported the Confederacy and outfitted the Prattville Dragoons. "I profess [he said] to be a Southern Rights man, and strongly contend that the South ought to maintain her rights at all hazards. I do this not as a politician but by aiding in the development of iron, coal, lime, and marble, and forest resources; by building railroads and manufacturing axes, hoes, spades, firearms, wagons, carriages, saddles and harness, window sashes and doors, and cotton gins."

The University of Alabama recognized Pratt's contributions to the state by bestowing upon him an honorary degree. In presenting the degree, President Basil Manly said; "Without having devoted your life to literary pursuits, you have attained in an eminent degree, that which is the end of all letters and study, the art of making all men around you wiser, better and happier. . . . Friend and supporter of schools for the son of the laboring man as well as the rich that all the rising generation may be fitted for that condition of republican freedom which is the peculiar privilege of Americans to enjoy."

William Kelly, a Pittsburgh, Pennsylvania, Yankee who had moved to Kentucky, developed the Bessemer process of making steel at his Eddyville, Kentucky, Iron Works, and paved the way for the age of steel. As a young man in Pittsburgh, Kelly had demonstrated his ingenuity by building a propelling waterwheel and a revolving steam engine. He had also established a successful commission house. When the latter was destroyed by fire, Kelly removed to Kentucky in 1845. He bought a small iron plant at Eddyville on the Cumberland River where he specialized in manufacturing sugar kettles for the Louisiana sugar growers. He

began experimenting in the decarbonization of iron by forc-
ing air through the molten metal, making possible the manufacture of inexpensive soft steel. He was successful and
secured a patent for his invention. With his air-blowing process, as it was locally called, Kelly and his partner built their
Iron Works and Union-Forge into one of the leading steel
plants in the country. Some time later Henry Bessemer of
England developed a process similar to that of Kelly's and
came to the United States to protest Kelly's claim. He
brought suit but the court upheld Kelly's patent in 1857.
Even so the process is now known as the Bessemer process.
However, a Yankee in the South had taken the first important step in the making of steel. As a result a considerable
iron and steel industry developed in the upper tier of Southern states. In 1859 Kelly built the first successful fitted steam
converter at his Cambrai Iron Works. He moved to Louisville, Kentucky, in 1861 and established an ax manufacturing plant. He died in 1881. Kelly was honored in 1925 by
the American Society for Steel Treating when it erected and
dedicated a bronze tablet to him at the Wyandott Iron
Works.

William H. Young, a native of New York, moved to Georgia in 1824 as the representative of a New York wholesale
clothing company. The company failed during the Panic of
1837, and Young and Dr. Henry Lockhart engaged in the
cotton export trade at Appalachicola, Florida, and made a
sizable fortune. Young settled at Columbus, Georgia, and
established a textile factory, the Eagle Wagon Factory, and
the Georgia Home Insurance Company. He was a loyal
supporter of the Confederacy and at a cost of $65,000 he
equipped a battery of artillery with uniforms, guns, and
horses. His entire business establishment was burned when
the Federal troops captured Columbus.

Yankees who were mechanics and common laborers made
important contributions to the development of Southern industry and transportation, but few of them left records of

their activities. One who did was James J. McCarter, a native of New Jersey who moved to Charleston, South Carolina, and worked as a mechanic. He wrote to a friend in New Jersey: "In that city I pulled off my coat, rolled up my sleeves, and in as public manner as the nature of my vocation admitted of, went to work. And I assure you, my friend, that in ten years I had attained to as high a social position as I could have reached in New Jersey in twenty years." Men are prone to exaggerate their accomplishments when they attempt to impress their friends, and certainly McCarter was no shrinking violet. But the truth is that he was not only a leader in the Charleston Mechanics Association but was also elected to membership in the South Carolina legislature from the city of Charleston.

Gail Borden, born in New York in 1801, migrated to Kentucky in 1815 where he was successively a farmer, schoolteacher, and surveyor. From Kentucky he moved to Mississippi, and then to Texas where he continued his work as a surveyor but turned primarily to stock raising. Borden made the first topographical map of Texas and also surveyed and laid out the city of Galveston. The need of good food on the frontier led Borden to experiment with the preservation of meats and he came up with concentrated meat biscuits. Col. E. V. Sumner of the United States Army, on duty in New Mexico, wrote to the War Department and said: "I have tried the 'Meat Biscuit' and found it all and more than the inventor thinks it is. I have lived upon it entirely for several days, and felt no want of any other food." Dr. Ashbel Smith of Texas wrote to Dr. Alexander Dallas Bache, president of the American Association for the Advancement of Science, enthusiastically endorsing the new invention and won his support. A patent was granted by the United States government on February 1, 1850. Today we enjoy the benefits of this Yankee inventive genius in the form of bouillon cubes, condensed milk, and concentrated fruit juices. Borden exhibited the meat biscuit at the London Fair of 1851, won a gold medal, and was elected to the London Society of Arts. On the return voyage he observed the lack of milk for children and turned his attention to that problem. In 1853 he developed the "process of evaporating milk in a vacuum," which was patented in 1856. Jeremiah Milbank furnished the money and built a factory for the production of evaporated milk in New York in 1861. The Civil War demonstrated the success of dry foods and the market was greatly expanded. Borden turned to the task of finding a satisfactory way of preserving fruits and in 1862 patented his process for concentrating "orange and other juices and fruits." Borden was much disturbed by secession and the Civil War. He wrote: "My best possessions are in Texas, that misguided State, where I had hoped to spend my last days; yet I love my whole country and government more, and wish to do what I can to sustain them." His brother Lee served in the Confederate Army, but Gail went to New York for the duration of the war. He returned to Texas in 1865 "and all but the most rabid Confederates welcomed him back to Texas as a brother, not a profiteering Yankee." Truly this Southern Yankee was a benefactor of mankind.

Transportation was an essential feature of the industrial revolution, and many Yankees played important roles in developing the transportation system of the Old South. Henry Miller Shreve, a New Jersey Yankee, did more to open steam navigation on the Mississippi River from St. Louis to New Orleans than any other person. In 1807 he had been the first to open river trade from Philadelphia by way of Pittsburgh to St. Louis. In 1810 he established the lead trade down the Mississippi to New Orleans. In 1814 he became part owner of the *Enterprise,* one of the first steamboats on the Mississippi, and performed valuable service for Gen. Andrew Jackson by running the British batteries and exchanging the prisoners of war. He then took the *Enterprise* upstream to Louisville, the first steamboat to ascend the river. He is also given the honor of having been the first to build staterooms on ships. Winston Churchill tells the story in *The Crisis* as follows: "There was an old fellow named Shreve before Jackson fought the redcoats at New Orleans. In Shreve's time cabins were curtained off . . . [but Shreve] built wooden rooms and named them after different States . . . and from this the name spread over the world—stateroom." In 1825 Secretary of War James Barber persuaded Shreve to accept the position of superintendent of western river improvements. At his own expense, but expecting repayment, Shreve built the *Heliopolis*, a strange looking vessel, which pulled up sawyers, logs, and trees from the riverbed. Shreve still did not get recompense and Capt. J. J. Albert of the United States Topographical Bureau wrote that the vessel *Uncle Sam's Tooth Puller* as it was called, was capable of removing snags and sawyers from the river and was indispensable. Shreve next removed the Grand Chain of Rocks in the Ohio and was then directed to attack the Great Raft, a raft of trees some 160 miles in length in the Red River. For this task Shreve designed and built the *Archimedes* with shallow draft for low water. The raft was completely removed in due time, and the city which grew up there was named Shreveport in honor of the man who had opened navigation on the river. At long last Shreve was officially commended: "Your ability, your zeal in public interest, your faithfulness in the execution of your tasks, entitle your conduct not only to an avowal of satisfaction but also an expression of high appreciation."

Lemuel P. Grant, a native of Maine, moved to Georgia in 1840 and found work as an engineer with the Georgia Railroad Company, of which he later became president. He was chief engineer for several Georgia railroads, including the Georgia, the Atlanta and West Point, the Atlanta and Montgomery, and the Georgia Pacific, which was to become an important link in the Southern Railway System. He opposed secession but actively supported the Confederacy. He was the engineer in charge of building the breastworks and fortifications around Atlanta behind which the Confederates for

a time held off Gen. William T. Sherman's army. Grant's
name is perpetuated in Atlanta in Grant's Park and other
monuments to his memory and philanthropy.

Norven Green, a native of Indiana, was a key figure in the
development of the telegraph in the Old South. In 1853 he
leased and consolidated the telegraph lines throughout the
lower Mississippi Valley and organized the Southwestern
Telegraph Company. He was among the first to conceive the
idea of consolidating all the lines in the United States, and
in 1857 he brought together the six leading companies in the
United States under the name of the North American Telegraph Company of which he became president. During the
Civil War the company was broken up, but in 1866 Green
brought about a larger consolidation—the Western Union
Telegraph Company. He served as vice president and president of the company until 1893.

Wealthy Yankee merchants contributed much to the social, cultural, civic, and economic life of the towns and cities
in which they lived. Enoch Pratt and Judah Touro are excellent examples of Yankee merchants in the Old South. Pratt
was born in Boston in 1808 and moved to Baltimore in 1830.
As an iron merchant he peddled his wares on the streets of
Baltimore, pushing his stock in a wheelbarrow. He prospered
and in 1831 established the Pratt Iron and Steel Company
which grew rapidly. Then followed fire insurance, a bank, a
shipping firm, railroads, canals, and other business enterprises. He amassed a fortune and spent it wisely and well for the
good of the people. He established the Peabody Institute and
contributed to a house of reform and instruction for Negro
children, the Maryland School for the Deaf and Dumb, an
asylum for mental patients, a nursery and children's hospi-
tal, and he donated a building to the Maryland Academy of
Science. Pratt detested slavery and characterized the institution as "an offense crying out to heaven." He advocated
freedom and education for the slave, and gave financial aid

to the American Colonization Society. He looked upon secession as a "social and political crime," and when the Civil
War came, he devoted his efforts to bring victory to the
Union. He made available to the United States government
the resources of his various industries, and he purchased
government bonds. After the war, he matured a plan which
he had long considered, namely, the establishment of a "free
circulating public library open to all regardless of color."
This, he said, was Baltimore's greatest need. He endowed the
Enoch Pratt Free Library with a million dollars. It was
opened in 1886.

Judah Touro was the foremost Yankee merchant-philan-
thropist in the Old South. His biographer said that Touro
"combined in delicate harmony the qualities of an American
Patriot and American gentleman with a deep devotion to his
ancestral faith and a broad toleration for other denominations." Born in Rhode Island in 1775, Touro removed to
New Orleans in 1801. He arrived in the city penniless, for
he had been robbed on his voyage to Louisiana. He engaged
in merchandising, the import-export trade, and real estate.
He served in the War of 1812 and was hospitalized for twelve
months. After the war his business enterprises flourished and
prospered, and he became one of the wealthiest citizens of
the state. He inherited $180,000 from his family in New
England, but immediately gave this sum to charity. Most of
his gifts were made privately for he disliked ostentation and
display. He gave freely to Jewish causes in Europe, Asia, and
China and to churches, hospitals, and asylums in the United
States. Among the local causes he supported were the Hebrew Benevolent Society, the New Orleans Free Library, the
Seamen's Home, and various synagogues, infirmaries, and
hospitals. He did not, however, limit his gifts to Jewish
groups. When the New Orleans Congregational Church, of
which Theodore Clapp, a New England Yankee, was the
minister, burned, Touro bought and gave another building

to the congregation. His will provided for the distribution of his entire fortune to benevolent causes. To the Hebrew congregation in New Orleans he left a synagogue, a residence for the rabbi, a schoolhouse, and an endowment to support both the rabbi and the teacher. He distributed the remainder of his estate to churches, schools, hospitals, asylums, orphans' homes, libraries and other worthy causes in thirteen states, seven of which were in the South. He also provided for schools, synagogues, and infirmaries in London and Jerusalem.

Touro died in New Orleans, January 18, 1854. The New Orleans *Bulletin* characterized him as one of the best men who ever lived: "He was foremost in improving the city, detested ostentation, but loved to do good in secret." The New Orleans *Delta* said, "New Orleans has lost one of her best citizens, charity one of her sincerest devotees, and humanity one of its truest friends." Pierce Butler characterized the career of Touro as one "so unobtrusive, so remarkable for the prosaic rarity of exact performance of daily duties; and yet one feels that the world somehow ought to be reproached because it took no note of one who wrought so much permanent good." Butler was incorrect, however, when he said the world took no note of what Touro had done. Memorials have been established for him in many cities in the United States, and Louisiana honored him by including him among the twenty-two greatest men in her history. Touro's statue appears on the front of the Louisiana State Capitol in recognition of his contributions to the state and her people.

A case study of Northerners in New Orleans in 1850 shows that of 40,000 American-born whites in the city 9,461 were Yankees by birth. Most of them had been born on farms in Massachusetts, New York, and Pennsylvania and had received a common school education. They had moved into the towns of their native states and had found employment in mercantile houses before they removed to New Orleans.

They seem to have had little interest in becoming planters for most of them became merchants, bankers, brokers, agents of Northern business houses, or journalists. James Robb's career was typical of those of many New Orleans Yankees. Born in Pennsylvania, he moved to New Orleans in 1837 with only a few hundred dollars in cash. He opened a brokerage office, weathered the financial crisis in 1837, and prospered. In 1840 he was co-founder of the banking firm of Robb and Hoge. He purchased nearly worthless stock in the New Orleans Gas Light and Banking Company and by good management made it profitable. He was the principal instigator of the New Orleans, Jackson, and Great Northern Railroad. He founded and was sole owner of the Bank of James Robb and established branches in St. Louis, San Francisco, New York, London, and Liverpool. He served as a member of the city council and as a state senator. He was a well-loved citizen, and his home was one of the showplaces in the city.

Yankees were also leaders in the economic and cultural life of New Orleans. The two coastal shipping lines were owned by Yankees, and the president of the Steam Tow-Boat Association was a Yankee. The city's leading bankers were Yankees. The three state banks—the Bank of Louisiana, the Louisiana State Bank, and the City Bank—were presided over by Yankees, and the chief executives of four of the eight local banks were Yankees. Several of the city newspapers were owned and edited by Yankees. The *Picayune,* largest of the city papers, was founded by a native of New Hampshire, and its editorial staff was largely made up of Northerners; the *Crescent* was founded by a popular Maine orator; and the *Commercial Bulletin* was founded by a native of Connecticut who was a graduate of Yale University.

From the early days of the United States, Yankees had moved into the Southern states and were generally accepted. At first they were somewhat opposed to slavery, but most of them gradually accepted the institution and many of them became ardent champions of slavery. A brief backward glance will show that the Southern Yankees, many of whom became wealthy merchants, bankers and planters, contributed much to the social, cultural, economic, and political life of the Old South. They visited the spas, the mountain resorts, and the theaters in the cities. Some of them became merchants and bankers and controlled commercial trade and the slave market. A goodly number married the daughters of Southern planters. The Yankee leaders also found their way into politics. They became members of the state legislatures, governors of states, or members of the United States Congress. Others were justices of the state courts, and some few became justices of the United States courts. The middle-class Yankee, like a Southerner, might find a place in various business enterprises. Other Yankees found an outlet in journalism, education, agriculture, and the clergy. This close relationship of Southerners and Yankees continued until the secession of the eleven states that formed the Confederate States of America. A large number of citizens of Maryland, Kentucky, and Missouri were loyal to the Confederacy.

Bibliography

I. Government and Politics

Abernethy, Thomas P. "The Origin of the Whig Party in Tennessee." *Mississippi Valley Historical Review* 12 (1926): 504–22.

Copeland, Fayette. *Kendall of the Picayune, Being His Adventures in New Orleans, on the Texan Santa Fe Expedition, in the Mexican War, and the Colonization of the Texas Frontier* (1943).

Evans, Harry H. "James Rabb, Banker and Pioneer Railroad Builder of Ante-Bellum Louisiana." *Louisiana History* 23 (1940): 170–258.

Farrand, Max. *Records of the Federal Convention* (1911).

Fulton, John F. *Benjamin Silliman 1779–1864: Pathfinder in American Science* (1947).

Hall, D. H., ed. "A Yankee Tutor [Charles W. Holbrook] in the Old South." *New England Quarterly* 32 (1960): 82–91.

Hall, Jerome. "Edward Livingston and His Penal Code." *American Bar Association Journal* 22 (1936): 191–96.

Holley, Mrs. Mary Austin. *Texas: Observations, Historical, Geographical and Descriptive. In a Series of Letters, Written during a Visit to Austin's Colony, with a View to a Permanent Settlement in That Country, in the Autumn of 1831. With an Appendix* (1933).

Hamilton, J. G. deRoulhac. "Southern Members of the Inns of Court." *North Carolina Historical Review* 10 (1933): 273–86.

Hatcher, William B. *Edward Livingston: Jeffersonian Republican and Jacksonian Democrat* (1940).

Hogan, William R. *The Texas Republic: A Social and Economic History* (1946).

Holmes, Alester G. *Thomas Green Clemson: His Life and Work* (1937).

Hutchinson, William T. *Seed-Time, 1809–1856. Cyrus Hall McCormick*, vol. 1. Reprint. (1968).

_____ . *Harvest, 1856–1884. Cyrus Hall McCormick*, vol. 2. Reprint. (1968).

Jones, Anson. *President of Texas* (1844).

Kendall, George Wilkins. *Narrative of the Texas Santa Fe Expedition.* 2 vols. (1844).

Lathrop, Barnes F. *Migrations into East Texas, 1835–1860: A Study from the United States Census* (1949).

McCain, William D. "The Adminstration of David Holmes, Governor of the Mississippi Territory, 1809–1817." *Journal of Mississippi History* 19 (1967): 328–47.

Niles, Hezekiah. *Principles and Acts of the Revolution in America.* Introduction by Henry Steele Commager (1965).

Prentice, George D. *Biography of Henry Clay* (1831).

Quitman, John A. C. *Life and Correspondence of John A. Quitman.* 2 vols. (1860).

Sears, Louis M. *John Slidell* (1925).

Semmes, John E. *John H. B. Latrobe and His Times, 1803–1891* (1917).

Shenton, James P. *Robert John Walker: A Politician, from Jackson to Lincoln* (1961).

Shields, J. D. *The Life and Times of Sergeant Smith Prentiss* (1884).

Sibley, Marilyn. *Travellers in Texas, 1761–1860* (1967).

Smith, Ashbel. *Reminiscences of the Texas Republic* (1876).

Smith, Eugene. "Edward Livingston and the Louisiana Code." *Columbia Law Review* 2 (1902): 24–36.

Smith, Justin H. *Annexation of Texas* (1911).

Sonne, Niels H. *Liberal Kentucky, 1780–1828* (1971).

Steel, Edward M. *Thomas Butler King of Georgia* (1964).

Van Buren, A. DePuy. *Jottings of a Year's Sojourn in the South; or, First Impressions of the Country and Its People; with a Glimpse of School Teaching in That Southern Land, and Reminiscences of Distinguished Men* (1859).

Watterson, Henry. *George Dennison Prentice: A Memorial Address* (1870).

Willson, Beckles. *John Slidell and the Confederates in Paris, 1862–1865* (1932).

Windrow, John E. *John Berrien Lindsley* (1938).

II. Educational Leaders

Abernethy, Thomas P. *Historical Sketch of the University of Virginia* (1948).

Adams, Herbert B. *The College of William and Mary: A Contribution to the History of Higher Education, with Suggestions for Its National Promotion* (1887).

Battle, Kemp P. *History of the University of North Carolina.* 2 vols. (1912).

Bone, Winstead P. *A History of Cumberland University, 1842–1935* (1935).

Bruce, Philip A. *History of the University of Virginia, 1819–1919; The Lengthened Shadow of One Man.* 2 vols. (1920–22).

Caldwell, Joseph. *Letters on Popular Education Addressed to the People* (1832).

Clark, Thomas D. *A History of Kentucky* (1937).

Callcott, George H. *A History of the University of Maryland* (1966).

Come, Donald R. "The Influence of Princeton University on Higher Education in the South Before 1825." *William and Mary Quarterly,* 3d ser., 2 (1945): 352–96.

Cooper, Thomas. *The Statutes At Large of South Carolina.* 5 vols.

Coulter, E. Merton. *College Life in the Old South* (1951).

Davenport, F. Garvin. *Cultural Life in Nashville on the Eve of the Civil War* (1941).

Easterby, James H. *A History of the College of Charleston, Founded 1770* (1935).

Eaton, Clement. *The Freedom-of-Thought Struggle in the Old South.* Rev. ed. (1969).

_____ . *The Growth of Southern Civilization, 1790–1860* (1961).

_____ . *The Mind of the Old South.* Rev. ed. (1971).

Floon, Howard R. *The South in Northern Eyes, 1831–1861* (1958).

Folmsbee, Stanley J. *East Tennessee University 1840–1879: Predecessor of the University of Tennessee* (1959).

_____ . *Blount College and East Tennessee College, 1794–1840: The First Predecessors of the University of Tennessee* (1946).

Garrett, Mitchel B. *Sixty Years of Howard College, 1842–1902* (1927).

Green, Edwin L. *A History of the University of South Carolina* (1916).

Hollis, Daniel W. *South Carolina College, 1801–1865* (1951).

Hopkins, James F. *The University of Kentucky: Origins and Early Years* (1951).

Parrington, Vernon L. "The Mind of the South." In *The Romantic Revolution in America, 1800–1860.* vol. 2, pp. 3–179 (1927).

Paschal, George W. *History of Wake Forest College.* Vol. 1, 1834–1865 (1935).

Peter, Robert. *History of the Medical Department of Transylvania University* (1905).

_____ . *Transylvania University: Its Origin, Rise, Decline, and Fall* (1896).

Postell, William D. "Louisiana; Its Record of Medical Progress, 1718–1860." *New Orleans Medical and Surgical Journal* 96 (1944): 530–36.

Sellers, James B. *History of the University of Alabama.* Vol. 1, 1818–1902 (1953).

Tankersley, Allen P. *College Life at Old Oglethorpe* (1951).

Tyler, Lyon G. *The College of William and Mary in Virginia: Its History and Work, 1693–1907* (1907).

Weathersby, William H. *A History of Educational Legislation in Mississippi from 1798 to 1860* (1921).

Woodrow, James. *Evolution* (1884).

Wright, Louis B. *Culture on the Moving Frontier* (1955).

III. Journalists, Humorists, and the Theatre

Abell, Arunah S. Baltimore *Sun*, 1837–1868.

Allan, Elizabeth Preston. *The Life and Letters of Margaret Junkin Preston* (1903).

Barnes, Eric W. *The Lady of Fashion: The Life and the Theatre of Ann Cora Mowatt* (1954).

Congleton, Betty Carolyn. "George D. Prentice: Nineteenth Century Southern Editor." *Register of the Kentucky Historical Society* 65 (1967): 94–119.

Crawford, Mary C. *The Romance of the American Theatre*. Boston (1913).

Dodd, William G. "Theatrical Entertainment in Early Florida." *Florida Historical Quarterly* 25 (1946): 121–74.

Dormon, James H., Jr. *Theater in the Ante-Bellum South, 1815–1861* (1967).

Eaton, Clement. "Winfred and Joseph Gales, Liberals in the Old South." *Journal of Southern History* (1944), pp. 461–74.

"George D. Prentice." *Register of the Kentucky Historical Society*, September 1915.

Gilman, Carolyn Howard. *Oracles from the Poets: A Fanciful Diversion for the Drawing Room* (1845).

———. *The Poetry of Traveling in the United States* (1838).

———. *Recollections of a New England Bride and Southern Matron*. 2d ed., rev. (1852).

Harris, George Washington. *Sut Lovingood Yarns* (1867).

Hayne, Barrie. "Yankee in the Patriarchy: T. B. Thorpe's Reply to Uncle Tom's Cabin." *American Quarterly* 20 (1968): 180–95.

Holmes, Francis S. *The Southern Farmer and Market Gardener: Being a Compilation of Useful Articles on These Subjects, from the Most Approved Writers*. Rev. ed. (1852).

Holmes, Mary Jane. *Tempest and Sunshine; or, Life in Kentucky* (1894).

Hoole, William S. *The Ante-Bellum Charleston Theatre* (1946).

Hornblower, Arthur. *A History of the Theatre in America from Its Beginnings to the Present Time* (1919).

Ingraham, Joseph Holt. *The Southwest by a Yankee*. 2 vols. (1835).

Kendall, George W. *Narrative of the Texan Santa Fe Expedition*. 2 vols. (1844).

Kendall, John S. *The Golden Age of the New Orleans Theater* (1952).

Kmen, Henry A. *Music in New Orleans: The Formative Years, 1791–1841* (1966).

Ludlow, Noah Miller, *Ludlow's Dramatic Life As I Found It: A Record of Personal Experience* (1880).

Luxon, N. Neal. *Niles' Weekly Register: News Magazine of the Nineteenth Century* (1947).

Meine, Franklin J., ed. *Tall Tales of the Southwest: An Anthology of Southern and Western Humor, 1830–1860* (1930).

Moses, Montrose J., and Brown, John M., eds. *The American Theatre As Seen by Its Critics, 1752–1934* (1934).

Niles, Hezekiah, ed. *Niles' Weekly Register.*

Pike, Albert. *Hymns to the Gods, and Other Poems.* 2 vols. (1882).

_____ . *Prose Sketches and Poems, Written in the Western Country.* David J. Weber, ed. (1967).

Prentice, George D., ed. *Prenticeiana* (1860).

Rankin, Hugh Z. *The Theatre in Colonial America* (1965).

Rickles, Milton. *George Washington Harris* (1965).

_____ . *Thomas Bangs Thorpe: Humorist of the Old Southwest* (1962).

Ritchie, Anna Cora Mowatt. *Plays by Anna Cora Mowatt* (1855).

Schmidt, Martin F. "The Early Printers of Louisville, 1800–1860." *Filson Club History Quarterly* 40 (1966): 307–34.

Shockley, Martin S. "American Plays in the Richmond Theater, 1819–1838." *Studies in Philology* 37 (1940): 100–119.

Smith, Soloman F., ed. *The Independent Press and Freedom's Advocate.*

_____ . *The Theatrical Apprenticeship and Anecdotal Recollections of Soloman Franklin Smith: A Sketch of the First Seven Years of His Life* (1846).

_____ . *The Theatrical Journey-Work and Anecdotal Recollections of Sol Smith, Comedian, Attorney at Law, etc., etc., Comprising a Sketch of Second Seven Years of His Professional Life; Together with Sketches of Adventure in After Years; With a Portrait of the Author* (1854).

_____ . *Theatrical Management in the West and South for Thirty Years. Inter-Sperced with Anecdotal Sketches: Autobiographically Given by Sol Smith, Retired Actor* (1868).

Stone, Richard G. *Hezekiah Niles as an Economist* (1933).

Thompson, William Tappan. *Major Jones' Chronicles of Pineville* (1843).

Thorpe, Thomas Bangs. *The Master's House: A Tale of Southern Life* (1854).

_____ . *The Mysteries of the Backwoods; or, Sketches of the Southwest: Including Characters, Scenery and Rural Sports* (1846).

Willis, Eola. *The Charleston Stage in the Eighteenth Century, with Social Settings of the Time* (1924).

Yates, Norris W. *William T. Porter and the Spirit of the Times: A Study of the Big Bear School of Humor* (1957).

IV. *Religious Leaders*

Bascom, Henry B. *Methodism and Slavery: With Other Matters in Controversy between the North and the South; Being a Review of the Manifesto of the Majority* (1845).

Cleveland, Catharine C. *The Great Revival in the West, 1797–1805* (1916).

Duffy, John, ed. *Parson Clapp of the Strangers' Church of New Orleans* (1957).

Gewehr, Wesley M. *The Great Awakening in Virginia, 1740–1790* (1930).

Gildersleeve, Basil L. *The Creed of the Old South* (1915).

Gildersleeve, Benjamin, ed. The Charleston *Observer* and the *Central Presbyterian*.

Hall, The Rev. James H. B. *The History of the Cumberland Presbyterian Church in Alabama prior to 1826* (1904).

Henkle, M. M. *Life of Henry B. Bascom* (1856).

History of the Baptist Denomination in Georgia with Biographical Compendium and Portrait Gallery of Baptist Ministers and Georgia Baptists. Compiled for *The Christian Index* (1881).

Johnson, Guion Griffis. "The Camp Meeting in Ante-Bellum North Carolina." *North Carolina Historical Review* 10 (1933): 95–110.

Matlock, Lucius C. *The History of American Slavery and Methodism, from 1780 to 1849 . . .* (1849).

Matthews, Donald G. *Slavery and Methodism: A Chapter in American Morality, 1780–1845* (1965).

Meinn, Joseph K. *The Large Slave Holders of Louisiana—1860* (1964)

Moore, John H. "The Abiel Abbot Journals: A Yankee Preacher in Charleston Society, 1818–1827." *South Carolina Historical Magazine* 68 (1967): 51–73; 115–39; 232–54.

Paschal, George W. *History of North Carolina Baptists.* 2 vols. (1930–1955).

Posey, Walter B. *The Baptist Church in the Lower Mississippi Valley, 1776–1845* (1957).

_____ . *The Development of Methodism in the Old Southwest, 1783–1824* (1933).

_____ . *Frontier Mission: A History of Religion West of the Southern Appalachians to 1861* (1969).

_____ . *The Presbyterian Church in the Old Southwest, 1778–1838* (1952).

_____ . "The Protestant Episcopal Church: An American Adaptation." *Journal of Southern History* 25 (1959): 3–30.

Putnam, Mary B. *The Baptists and Slavery, 1840–1845* (1913).

Semple, Robert B. *A History of the Rise and Progress of the Baptists in Virginia* (1810).

Sherwood, Adiel. *Baptist Triennial Convention* (1823).

_____ , comp. *A Gazetteer of the State of Georgia* (1939).

Shipp, Albert M. *The History of Methodism in South Carolina* (1883).

Sweet, William W. *Methodism in American History*. Rev. ed. (1954).

_____ . *The Methodist Episcopal Church and the Civil War* (1912).

_____ , ed. *The Presbyterians, 1783–1840: A Collection of Source Materials* (1936).

_____ , ed. *Religion on the Frontier: The Baptists, 1783–1830. A Collection of Source Material*. Introduction by Shirley J. Case (1931).

_____ , ed. *The Rise of Methodism in the West: Being the Journal of the Western Conference, 1800–1811* (1920).

Thompson, Ernest T. *Presbyterians in the South, 1607–1861* (1963).

Walker, Joseph L., ed. *Baptist Champion, Baptist Recorder,* and *Christian Index*.

V. *Agriculturalists and Industrialists*

Affleck, Thomas, ed. *Plantation Book* (1847).

Bonner, James C. *A History of Georgia Agriculture, 1732–1860* (1964).

_____ , ed. "Plantation Experiences of a New York Woman." *North Carolina Historical Review* 33 (1956): 384–412; 529–46.

Davis, Edwin A. "Bennet H. Barrow, Ante–Bellum Planter of the Felicians." *Journal of Southern History* 5 (1939): 431–46.

Downing, Andrew J. *Fruit and Fruit Trees of America; or, The Culture, Propagation and Management, in the Garden and Orchard.* . . . Charles Downing, ed. 2d rev. ed. (1882).

Gara, Larry, ed. "A New Englander's View of Plantation Life; Letters of Edwin Hall to Cyrus Woodman, 1837." *Journal of Southern History* 18 (1952): 343–54.

Gray, Lewis C. *History of Agriculture in the Southern States to 1860.* 2 vols. Reprint (1941).

Green, Norven. *The Government and the Telegraph: An Article Contributed to the North American Review for November, 1883; with Supplement and Appendix, Showing Reflex of Newspaper Criticism* (1833).

House, Albert V., ed. *Plantation Management and Capitalism in Ante-Bellum Georgia: The Journal of Hugh Fraser Grant, Rice Grower* (1954).

Hungerford, Edward. *The Story of the Baltimore & Ohio Railroad, 1827–1927.* 2 vols. (1928).

Jordan, Weymouth T. "Noah B. Cloud's Activities on Behalf of Southern Agriculture." *Agricultural History* 25 (1951): 53–58.

Kellar, Herbert A., ed. *Solon Robinson, Pioneer and Agriculturist: Selected Writings, 1825–1851.* 2 vols. (1936).

Latrobe, John H. B. *The First Steamboat Voyage on the Western Waters* (1871).

Olmsted, Denison. "Report on the Geology of North Carolina, Conducted Under the Direction of the Board of Agriculture." *Southern Review* (1828), pp. 235–61.

Peabody, Charles Albert, ed. *The Soil of the South* and *The American Cotton Planter.*

Roland, Charles P. *Louisiana Sugar Plantations during the American Civil War* (1957).

Scarborough, William K. *The Overseer: Plantation Management in the Old South* (1966).

Simons, A. M., ed. *The American Farmer* (1902).

Thompson, Robert L. *Wiring a Continent: The History of the Telegraph Industry in the United States from 1832 to 1866* (1947).

Ward, G. W. *The Early Development of the Chesapeake and Ohio Canal Project* (1899).

VI.   *Biography.*

Allsopp, Frederick W. *Albert Pike: A Biography* (1928).

Bachman, John. *The Doctrine of the Unity of the Human Race Examined on the Principle of Science* (1850).

_____ . *The Unity of the Human Race* (1855).

Barker, Eugene C. *The Life of Stephen F. Austin, Founder of Texas, 1793–1836: A Chapter in the Westward Movement of the Anglo-American People* (1968).

Barker, Eugene C., and Williams, Amelia W., eds. *The Writings of Sam Houston, 1813–1863* (1938–1943).

Baughman, James P. "A Southern Spa: Ante-Bellum Lake Pontchartrain." *Louisiana History* 3 (1962): 5–32.

Bolzau, Emma L. *Almira Hart Lincoln Phelps: Her Life and Work* (1936).

Boucher, John N. *William Kelly: A True History of the So-Called Bessemer Process* (1924).

Clapp, Theodore. *Autobiographical Sketches and Recollections, during a Thirty-Five Years' Residence in New Orleans.* 2d ed. (1858).

Clarkson, Paul S., and Jett, R. Samuel. *Luther Martin of Maryland* (1969).

Comfort, Harold W. *Gail Borden and His Heritage since 1857* (1953).

Cook, Harvey T. *A Biography of Richard Furman* (1913).

Delapaine, Edward C. *The Life of Thomas Johnson: Member of the Continental Congress, First Governor of the State of Maryland, and an Associate Justice of the United States Supreme Court* (1927).

Dickey, Dallas C. *Sergeant S. Prentiss: Whig Orator of the Old South* (1945).

Dodd, William E. *Robert J. Walker, Imperialist.* Reprint. (1967).

Dorsey, Florence L. *Master of the Mississippi: Henry Shreve and the Conquest of the Mississippi* (1941).

Drake, Daniel. *Pioneer Life in Kentucky; A Series of Reminiscent Letters.* Charles D. Drake, ed. (1870).

Gambrell, Herbert P. *Anson Jones: The Last President of Texas.* Foreword by William R. Hogan. 2d ed. (1964).

Hamlin, Talbot F. *Benjamin Henry Latrobe* (1955).

Hanaford, Phebe Ann. *The Life of George Peabody, Containing a Record of Those Princely Acts of Benevolence which Entitle Him to the Esteem and Gratitude of All Friends of Education and the Destitute* (1870).

Hart, Richard H. *Enoch Pratt: The Story of a Plain Man* (1935).

Hatcher, William B. *Edward Livingston: Jeffersonian Republican and Jacksonian Democrat* (1940).

Horine, Emmett F. *Biographical Sketch and Guide to Writings of Charles Caldwell, M. D. (1772–1853), with Sections on Phrenology and Hypnotism* (1960).

_____. *Daniel Drake, 1785–1852: Physician of the Mid-West.* Introduction by J. Christian Bay (1961).

Hosach, David. *A Biography: Memoir of Hugh Williamson* (1820).

Hühner, Leon. *The Life of Judah Tours, 1775–1854* (1946).

Ingraham, Joseph H. *Lafitte: The Pirate of the Gulf.* 2 vols. (1836).

Jones, C. C. *Biographical Sketches of the Delegates from Georgia to the Constitution Convention* (1891).

Kienzle, George J. *The Story of Gail Borden: The Birth of Industry* (1947).

Latrobe, Benjamin H. *Impressions Respecting New Orleans: Diary and Sketches 1818–1820.* Samuel Wilson, Jr., ed. (1951).

Latrobe, Benjamin Henry, ed. *The Journal of Latrobe, Being the Notes and Sketches of an Architect, Naturalist and Traveler in the United States from 1796 to 1820.* J. H. B. Latrobe, ed. (1905).

Lee, Rebecca S. *Mary Austin Holley, A Biography* (1962).

Nash, Francis. *Governor Alexander Martin: An Address* (1908).

Prentiss, G. L. *A Memoir of Sergeant S. Prentiss.* 2 vols. (1855).

Ripley, Eliza M. *Social Life in New Orleans, Being Recollections of My Girlhood* (1912).

Shippee, Lester B., ed. *Bishop Whipple's Southern Diary, 1843–1844* (1968).

Smith, Ashbel. *Autobiography* (1859).

Smith, Joseph F. *White Pillows; Early Life and Architecture in the Lower Mississippi Valley Country* (1941).

Tarrant, Susan F. *Hon. Daniel Pratt: A Biography with Eulogies on His Life and Character* (1904).

Tope, Mellancthan. *A Biography of William Homes McGuffey* (1929).

Watson, I. A. *Physicians and Surgeons of America* (1896).

White, Henry C. *Abraham Baldwin: One of the Founders of the Republic, and Father of the University of Georgia* (1926).

Index